Melting ice on Loch Ba, Rannoch Moor

Scots Pines at Dunadd, seat of the Kings of Dalriada

ROB ROY'S COUNTRY

For Gregor

First published 2003 by

SCOTTISH CULTURAL PRESS

Unit 13d, Newbattle Abbey Business Annexe
Newbattle Road, DALKEITH EH22 3LJ Scotland
Tel: +44 (0)131 660 6366 • Fax: +44 (0)131 660 4666
Email: info@scottishbooks.com
www.scottishbooks.com

*Note: the map on page 28 should be viewed as a guide to Rob Roy's Country;
it is not intended as an exact representation of the area*

BRITISH LIBRARY CATALOGUING IN PUBLICATION DATA
A catalogue record for this book is available from the British Library

ISBN: 1 84017 048 4

Printed and bound by Bell & Bain Ltd, Glasgow

Rob Roy's Country

Mary McGrigor

with photographs by

Malcolm MacGregor

Scottish Cultural Press

CONTENTS

Her Grace Iona, Duchess of Argyll

Could anything be more appropriate than this book about the most famous of Clan Gregor's sons – having been written by a McGrigor and photographed by Sir Malcolm MacGregor of MacGregor, Chief of Clan Gregor. Mary McGrigor is steeped in the knowledge of the legends and lores of this Scottish hero whose daring deeds have been written and sung about for over three centuries.

She brings alive every ruined castle and shieling, every hiding place and cave, and imbues them with her love of the Highlands and knowledge of Rob Roy's dealings with the nefarious nobles of the day.

These stories of bravery and treachery, combined with Mary's detailed and factual accounts of the places and country known to Rob Roy and his associates, will make this a fascinating read to all who love the Highlands and especially to those who walk the West Highland Way. She has unearthed in our lonely glens and rugged country tales of derring-do and acts of clan greed and aggression. These are the heroic legends of the 'Children of the Mist', recounted with imagination and an eye for detail. They come from a period of Scottish history when the clans were at their most turbulent and the pen had not yet overtaken the sword; when Scotland was traversed by drove roads known only to the reivers, before the coming of General Wade's military roads.

Malcolm MacGregor has re-traced these old routes, spending days and nights on the majestic mountains to capture the magic of the ever-changing Highland light. Through his photographs, the wild magnificence of Rob Roy's Country springs into the mind's eye. One can picture Rob Roy himself, wrapped in his plaid, sleeping under the stars, or striding behind a herd of cattle over now near-forgotten tracks.

Iona Argyll.

PHOTOGRAPHER'S NOTE

As a photographer, connecting landscape to the story of one of Scotland's most renowned historical figures demanded a new perspective. The hills and glens of Scotland were very different in the days of Rob Roy but the more remote areas have remained virtually the same, so this is what I concentrated on; being conscious of the need to recreate a feeling for the sort of country that was part of his life.

His times are associated with some of the most wild, remote and beautiful areas of the Highlands of Scotland. Rob Roy's knowledge of the terrain and his ability to move over it was second to none. Clambering around the high tops of Perthshire and Argyll, one could imagine him moving with his men swiftly and sure-footedly over those barren rocks. These magnificent mountains and glens were part of his being.

Although Rob Roy would have relied on his intuition and sense of direction to traverse the hills, for today's photographer maps are important. Viewpoints and locations can be identified for photography and the sun's position can be ascertained for a given time of the day. Much of the time was spent camping out in order to be in the best position to capture the light of a rising or setting sun. All equipment was carried in a small pack, which in turn was carried in a much larger back-pack that also contained warm clothing, bivi bag and food.

It is one thing to take a photograph that is technically good, but it is quite another to bring an 'added plus' to it, making the image something more than a snapshot. Some of the locations in this book were visited two or three times in order to get that 'added plus'. Returning to an area can be a good thing as you look at it in a different way and see other possibilities.

All the photographs in this book were done with a Mamiya 7 II medium format camera always mounted on a tripod. I have a carbon fibre and a heavier metal tripod. Carbon fibre is excellent, but is not steady enough in strong winds. It is always a fine judgement as to which tripod to carry, weight versus stability dependent on weather conditions.

I use four prime lenses; from ultra wide angle to short telephoto. Using only these lenses helps previsualisation as only those compositions are imprinted on my mind. Film stock was Fuji Velvia, a fine grain 50 asa film. Many of the photographs were done with filters. Neutral Density Grey Graduated which are essential for images with strong skies, Warm Ups (81a & 81c) for overcast weather and the Polariser for shots involving water or strong clouds. It is better to really understand a few filters and what they do, than to have an array which adds to the weight of an already full camera bag.

The best time to photograph in Scotland is in spring – days are getting longer and the weather is generally fine with consistently good light. Winter is over, but snow still lies on the tops and everything is crisp and coming to life. The air is fresh and clean with a distinctive highland odour that uplifts the heart and sets the mind thinking of a myriad of possibilities. Landscape photography not only provides a sense of freedom and exhilaration, but in the Highlands something else takes over one's motivations, being mindful of the tragic nature of its history. However, the story of Rob Roy is different; it is colourful, heroic, steeped in legend and lore, much like the country he inhabited.

INTRODUCTION

The eagle flies high above Ben Lomond. Behind his head and ferocious bill, his neck gleams golden in the sun. He soars on mighty wings, six feet from tip to tip. The kingdom of the sky his own.

Below him lies the heartland of the Highlands, where, two and half centuries ago, Rob Roy MacGregor knew every hill and glen. The long stretch of Loch Lomond, today lies calm beneath a cloudless sky. The trees of the east shore are mirrored on the surface of the water, unbroken except by the circle of ripples of a rising fish. Among those trees, on the bank above, was the farming township of Inversnaid where Rob Roy and his wife Helen Mary once lived. The walls of their house, blackened twice by fire when troops were sent to evict them, have now long disappeared. Over the Ben lies the Comer, the place where Helen Mary was born.

From his height, the eagle can trace the pass from the head of the Inversnaid burn down into Glengyle. Here, at the head of Loch Katrine, the boy called Rob Roy because of his red hair was born in 1671. At that time the mouth of Glengyle was good grazing. Since Loch Katrine became a reservoir for Glasgow, however, it lies beneath water.

Portnellan, on the north-east side of Loch Katrine, is where many MacGregors are buried. From here an old track leads over the watershed to the Inverlochlarig burn. Rob Roy's home in his later years was the farm near the foot of the glen called Inverlochlarig Beag. Heading east from there through the birch covered Braes of Balquhidder, by Loch Doine and Loch Voil, the road runs to the old village of Kirkton. There lies the grave of Rob Roy, his wife, Helen Mary, and two of their sons, close to the old parish church.

As a young man, Rob Roy thought nothing of walking fifty miles or more. The passes, the caves, the wide stretches of moorland were all imprinted on his mind. His vast knowledge of the country and local contacts were akin to a personal intelligence network. Herdsmen, innkeepers and itinerant pedlars passed on the news of what was currently afoot.

The eagle soars upwards, so high that in the far distance he can see the outline of the mountains above Glen Shiel, the 'Five Sisters of Kintail'. Beyond them, like clouds on the horizon, loom the massive Cuillins of Skye. Closer, to the north-west of Loch Lomond, beyond the jagged crown of the Cobbler, a silver streak of water, stretching like an arm from the sea, is Loch Fyne. Near the head of the loch, a short way from Inveraray, the tree-dark line of Glen Shira runs north up to *Beinn Bhuidhe*, yellow as is its Gaelic name beneath the summer sun. Beside the burn, in a hollow, hidden even from the eagle's eye, stand the walls of the cottage which Rob Roy was given by 'Red John of the Battles', a man after his own heart, the second Duke of Argyll.

Just beyond the watershed at the head of the glen, over the *Bealach nan Cabrach*, or 'Pass of the Antler', is Brackley, the farm above the old village of Clachan Dysart (now Dalmally) which Rob Roy once rented from the Earl of Breadalbane. It was because this great Campbell chief befriended him, each to the other's gain, that Rob Roy called himself Campbell when his own name of MacGregor was proscribed.

How much have these parts of Scotland changed in the course of over three hundred years? Would Rob Roy still recognise these same surroundings were he to return today?

He would certainly know the landmarks, the lochs, the rivers and the bens. Cruachan, Ben Lomond, Ben Ledi, Ben Lawers and the mighty Schiehallion – mountains which, even in his time, were old beyond the ken of mortal man. Also the Moor of Rannoch, that sinister stretch of water and peat, remains little unchanged. What memories would come back to him! How many anecdotes of past escapes and adventures would he re-live!

Uppermost in his mind would be the nights in caves or on the hillside, sleeping wrapped in his plaid. For three years, while pursued as an outlaw, he spent hardly more than a night in one place. This, he told the Duke of Atholl, was how he had been forced to exist. Their meeting at Dunkeld House, on 4 June 1717, resulted in one of Rob Roy's most famous escapades.

The story goes that Rob Roy, enticed to the Duke's residence by the hope of a reprieve, was instead imprisoned. After his ingenious escape, Rob Roy leapt on a horse's back and rode at a mad gallop to find safety once more among the hills.

How different are those hills today? What would Rob Roy think and feel if he were to see them once more? Doubtless, his first reaction would be a great shaking of the head. 'Such a great waste o' good grazing. It's no place the now for the kye.'

Since the time of his youth, in the latter part of the 1700s, the Highlands of Scotland have seen two major changes. Firstly, the introduction of large flocks of sheep and secondly, the planting of conifers on a vast scale.

Rob Roy grew up in an age when every bit of ground that could be dug with a spade, a caschrom or a plough was cultivated. Even patches by the burns were turned over for potatoes, corn and bear – the oats used for making ale, the staple drink of the country.

Also there were the stills. Nothing makes better whisky than grain distilled in the water of a clear Highland burn. There were, of course, the Excisemen to contend with – worthies like Rob's contemporary Robert Burns – but few were brave enough to risk a dirk at their throats in the wilds of the Highland hills.

What of those great peaks rising above the sheltered corries so much beloved of cattle and deer. How have they changed?

Certainly in the summer months, from May until October, they were greener. Sheep had only just been introduced to the Highlands – flocks of the great Cheviots and Blackfaces so detested by Gaelic poet of Rob Roy's time, Duncan Ban MacIntyre. He saw them as locusts, destroying the ancient pastures because, unlike cattle, they graze grass down to its roots.

Rob Roy MacGregor, descended from a son of King Alpin, was essentially a Highlander and, as such, was a cattle man. He was born and bred amongst the short hardy animals, the mainstay of existence and of currency since long forgotten time. No one had a better eye for a beast than he – what he would have thought of the dairy products of today's supermarket is probably better unknown!

Although the lower slopes of the hillsides in his day were largely covered in scrub, the huge stretches of conifers that now stretch up to fifteen hundred feet above sea-level would not have been pleasing to his eye. Useful they maybe for some purposes, profitable perhaps for a few, he would probably have thought them a sacrilege, a destruction of good open ground.

Perhaps he would have been most astounded by modern methods of transport. He who knew nothing faster than a horse and to whom every track across the hills was familiar, would have marvelled at, and most probably derided, the ease in which most of us travel today. He might, in fact, have pitied us, for how much have we lost? Only the hill-walkers and shepherds, the men of the mountains, have seen the magic of an early summer morning when deer move silently across the skyline in the dawn.

Rob Roy knew every part of this country in which he was born and lived and died. Perhaps his spirit still lingers like the mist which fades in the heat of the sun from the high tops of the hills.

MacGregor's Gathering

SIR WALTER SCOTT

The moon's on the lake, and the mist's on the brae,
And the clan has a name that is nameless by day.

Then gather, gather, gather, Gregarach!
Gather, gather, gather.

Our signal for fight, which from monarchs we drew,
Must be heard but by night in our vengeful haloo,

Then haloo, haloo, haloo, Gregarach!
Haloo, haloo, haloo.

Glenorchy's proud mountains, Kilchurn and her towers.
Glenstrae and Glen Lyon no longer are ours.

We're landless, landless, landless, Gregarach!
Landless, landless, landless.

But doomed and deserted by vassal and lord,
MacGregor has still both his heart and his sword.

Then courage, courage, courage, Gregarach!
Courage, courage, courage.

If they rob us of name and pursue us with beagles,
Give their roofs to the flames and their flesh to the eagles.

Then vengeance, vengeance, vengeance, Gregarach!
Vengeance, vengeance, vengeance.

While there's leaves in the forest and foam on the river,
MacGregor, despite them, shall flourish forever.

Come then, Gregarach! Come then, Gregarach!
Come then, come then, come then.

Through the depths of Loch Katrine the steed shall career,
O'er the peak of Ben Lomond the gallery shall steer,
And the rocks of Craigrostan like icicles melt,
Ere our wrongs be forgot or our vengeance unfelt.

Then haloo, haloo, haloo, Gregarach!
Haloo, haloo, haloo.

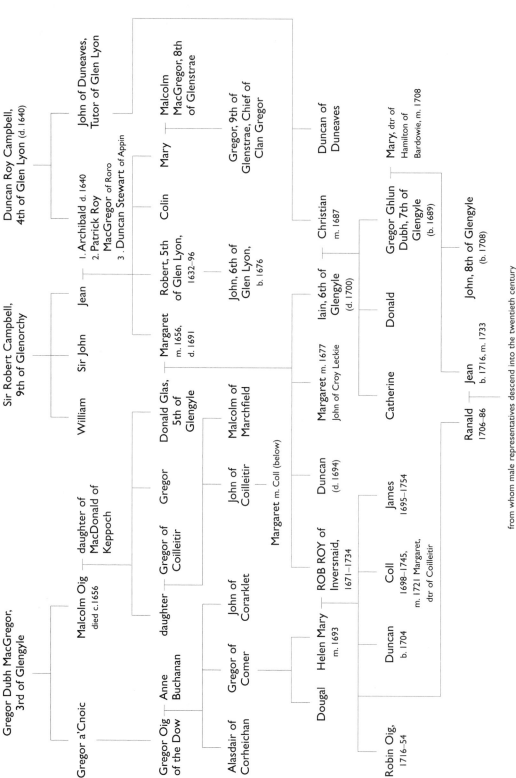

from whom male representatives descend into the twentieth century

Falls on the River Orchy, Argyll

Kilchurn Castle on Loch Awe, surrounded by the hills of Glen Lochy and Glen Orchy

Dalmally Church, burial place of the
chiefs of Clan Gregor

Glengyle with Loch Katrine in the distance

CHAPTER I

The Cradle of Clan Gregor

Glenorchy, Glenstrae and Glen Lochy

Some ten thousand years ago, a great sheet of ice began to melt on Rannoch Moor. The water gouged out riverbeds in its path to the south west. The River Orchy, from Loch Tulla, descends slowly at first and then flows down waterfalls and through deep pools to the floor of the glen. Here it is joined first by the Lochy and then, beyond Dalmally, by the Strae. Thus the flow of three rivers converge upon the east end of Loch Awe.

Prior to the last Ice Age, Loch Awe ran from its west end through the Eurach Gorge to the Sound of Jura, but the outflow became blocked by silt. Melting ice forced its way through the natural crack of the Pass of Brander until the pent-up water of Loch Awe poured through to form the River Awe, which runs north west to Loch Etive and the sea.

Gradually, as the ice melted, indigenous seeds which had lain buried beneath the permafrost, germinated and began to grow. First mosses, then grass and reeds, then willows and other native bushes and trees covered the ground. Bands of hunters from Europe landed on the coast perhaps as long ago as 7000 BC. They made their way up the lochs and rivers to make temporary settlements and eventually some of them remained.

A large contingent of people from Ireland, who arrived about 500 AD, established the kingdom of Dal Riata[1] centred near Crinan on the River Add. The Celtic King Alpin, who lived in the ninth century, is reputedly the ancestor of the people of Clan Gregor, who are sometimes known as the Clan Alpin to this day.

Miss Amelia MacGregor, in her *History of Clan Gregor* writes: 'Gregor was the third son of King Alpin and brother to Kenneth,

Donald and Achaius MacAlpin, the two former of whom reigned successively, *inter annos 834 et 859.'*

Sometime during the later part of the thirteenth century Malcolm MacGregor of Glenorchy married Marjory, daughter of William, Earl of Murray, and granddaughter of King Malcom II. A man of incredible strength, Malcolm MacGregor reputedly saved the life of one of the Scottish kings by tearing up a young oak tree and beating off a wild boar which was about to kill him. The monarch he saved (either Alexander I, David I or Malcolm IV) in gratitude made him a 'mormer', or peer, and is said to have given him an oak tree in place of the original armorial bearing of a fir tree. Today, the arms of the present chief bear an oak tree, while the fir remains on those of other branches of the clan.

Sir Malcolm was also called *Moref hir Callum nan Caistel* or 'Lord of the Castles' because he built so many strongholds. Among them was the first *Caol-Charn* (Kilchurn) at the north-east end of Loch Awe. Sir Malcolm died in 1164.[2]

His great-grandson, also Malcolm of Glenorchy, supported King Robert the Bruce during Scotland's War of Independence. During the fierce struggle at *Dal Righ* (near Tyndrum) between the king and the MacDougalls of Lorn, Malcolm is said to have charged into the heat of the battle, riding a milk-white horse. Bruce was defeated and escaped across the hills to MacGregor's lands, near Craigrostan on Loch Lomond, where he hid in *Uamh an Riogh*, 'The King's Cave'.

Malcolm fought again for Robert the Bruce at the Battle of Bannockburn in 1314. This time the Scots were victorious and it is said that Malcolm brought the relics of St Fillan from the battlefield to the king's chaplain. King Robert, believing a miracle had occurred, subsequently founded a priory in Strathfillan, then part of Malcolm MacGregor's land.

Later, in Ireland, the MacGregor chief fought under the king's brother, Edward Bruce. He was wounded in the leg at the Battle of Dundalk in 1318 and thereafter, walking with a limp, was known as *morfhear bachdach* or the 'lame lord'.[3]

Despite this, Malcolm died an old man in 1374.

Glenorchy

The glen of the River Orchy, is one of the most beautiful in Scotland. The river runs from Loch Tulla, below the Black Mount, and at first drops slowly in a series of long pools. Once the Scots pines of the Old Caledonian Forest grew here but they were felled in the late eighteenth century to leave open ground. This was the land of the Fletchers (the name derives from *Mac-an-leisdears*), the hereditary arrow-makers of the MacGregors, who claim to have been the first people to raise smoke to boil water in Glenorchy.[4]

Below Bridge of Orchy the river narrows into a ravine, before plunging over waterfalls. Then, as it nears its confluence with the Lochy, it flows through a wider course. The Orchy was one of the best salmon rivers in Scotland, renowned for its 'spring run'. Unfortunately, this has all but ended since the building of the Hydro-Electric barrage on the River Awe in the 1960s, which, in spite of a salmon lift, restricts the natural access of the fish.

From Bridge of Lochy the river continues through a green strath to reach the old village of Dysart, now known as Dalmally. The original village was centred round an island in the River Orchy upon which stood the early church. The white-painted tower of the Parish Church of Glenorchy (built *c.*1810) stands on the same site, although the island has since merged with the mainland. The tombs of the Chiefs of the MacGregors, who were buried here within the church, have now vanished, but grave-slabs of the medieval period, attributed to them, lie in the north-west corner of the churchyard. John MacGregor, grandson of Malcolm, the lame lord, is the first chief of the MacGregors known to have been buried in the church of Dysart, as it was then called.

John MacGregor's obituary, known as the 'Chronicle of Fortingal', gives the following:

> 1390, April 19th. Died John, son of Gregor of Glenurquhay [*sic*], and was buried in Dysart north of the High Altar. John, son of Gregor, was named *Cham*, or 'blind of an eye'.[5]

John MacGregor's eldest son, Gregor, known as Gregor *Aulin* (handsome), succeeded him. John's second son, again called John, was the progenitor of the MacGregors of Glenstrae, but it is his youngest son, named Dugald *Ciar*, who was the ancestor of the MacGregors of Glengyle and therefore of Rob Roy.

During the fourteenth century, the MacGregors, for their loyalty to the Scottish kings, became tenants of Crown lands. Unfortunately, they did not receive the charters of possession which became increasingly essential in the ensuing years. During the reigns of James III and IV, the lack of this formal agreement meant they lost not only the lordship of Glendochart, but other lands, including Glen Lyon, the Port of Loch Tay, the country of Rannoch and the barony of Finlarig.

Sir Duncan Campbell of Loch Awe, created Lord Campbell by King James II, was the King's Lieutenant in Argyll. A charter proves that he granted the superiority of Glenorchy to Colin, eldest son of his second marriage, in 1432. The fact that he retained the superiority of Glenstrae in his own hands, so that it descended to the Earls of Argyll, proved to be of great significance to the the MacGregors of Glenstrae.

Glenstrae

The burn becomes a river as it descends from *Beinn a' Chuirn*. It then threads its way between the mighty mountains of *Beinn Mhic Monaidh* on the south-east and *Beinn Larachan* on the north-west.

The upper strath of the glen is beloved of cuckoos in May. Today it is deserted, save for sheep, deer and nesting birds. No more is heard the lowing of cattle, the frantic barking of dogs, or the clamour of people herding their beasts up to the *airidhs*, or high pastures. The summer scent of thyme and the laughter of bare-footed children playing in the burn, guddling for trout and minnows, have long since disappeared. Shielings, greatly ruined, stand as testament to the bustle of life that once thrived in this sheltered, fertile landscape.

The burn, joined by others, becomes a river as it weaves its lonely way. In dry weather, the water runs clear as diamonds over a gravel bed. Only after heavy rain, or at times of melting snow, does it become a brown torrent, hurtling downwards between its banks.

Glenstrae, seen from a distance on a sunlit day, shines like a green snake, curving between the stark sides of the mountains through which it winds. At its foot, just above the road bridge, was the market of Rob Roy's day. Nearby, at the foot of *Beinn Eunaich*, a fortalice of 'Malcolm of the Castles' is believed to have been built, close to where the white-washed farmhouse called 'Castles' stands today.

The MacGregors of Glenstrae

The chiefs of Clan Gregor, vassals of Argyll from 1432, were enfeoffed[6] by their Campbell overlord on inheritance or, in the case of minority, upon their coming of age. They were proud men of strong character, who appear to have paid no more than lip-service to authority of any kind.

Iain Dubh, the 6th chief of Glenstrae, died in 1519. He was buried, like his forefathers, in a stone coffin within the walls of the old Church of Dysart. However, on the day of the funeral, a great meteor was seen in Glenorchy. Men foretold disaster and then later, when Iain Dubh's son was disinherited by the 3rd Earl of Argyll, claimed the prophesy had been fulfilled. 'From that day came the sad division and sorrows of the Gregarach, for the Campbells now enfeoffed his second cousin in his place.'

The usurper in question was John McEwan Vic Allastair (great grandson of John Dhu McEan *Cham*), who was styled 'Captain of the Clan Gregor'. John had ravished and then married a daughter of Sir Colin Campbell, 6th of Glenorchy ('Grey Colin'), and for this reason may have been chosen by the Campbells to supersede his cousin, the rightful heir.

~ GENEALOGY OF CLAN GREGOR ~

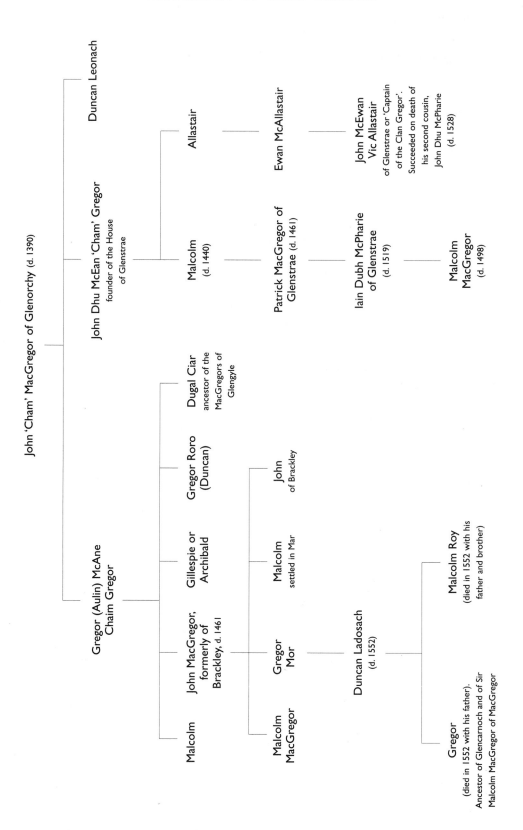

John 'Cham' MacGregor of Glenorchy (d. 1390)

Duncan Leonach

John Dhu McEan 'Cham' Gregor
founder of the House
of Glenstrae

Gregor (Aulin) McAne
Chaim Gregor

Allastair

Malcolm
(d. 1440)

Ewan McAllastair

Patrick MacGregor of
Glenstrae (d. 1461)

John McEwan
Vic Allastair
of Glenstrae or 'Captain
of the Clan Gregor'.
Succeeded on death of
his second cousin,
John Dhu McPharie
(d. 1528)

Iain Dubh McPharie
of Glenstrae
(d. 1519)

Malcolm
MacGregor
(d. 1498)

Dugal Ciar
ancestor of the
MacGregors of
Glengyle

Gregor Roro
(Duncan)

John
of Brackley

Gillespie or
Archibald

John MacGregor,
formerly of
Brackley, d. 1461

Malcolm
settled in Mar

Malcolm

Gregor
Mor

Duncan Ladosach
(d. 1552)

Malcolm Roy
(died in 1552 with his
father and brother)

Malcolm
MacGregor

Gregor
(died in 1552 with his father).
Ancestor of Glencarnoch and of Sir
Malcolm MacGregor of MacGregor

Kilchurn Castle

The east tower, or hall-house, four storeys high, and the curtain wall surrounding the castle were built by Sir Colin Campbell, 1st of Glenorchy, *c.*1440. It stands on the site of an earlier castle of the MacGregors, attributed to 'Malcolm of the Castles', who 'flourished in the reign of Alexander III'.

Sir Colin Campbell, 6th of Glenorchy ('Grey Colin'), rebuilt the top of the tower-house and added the corbelled angle rounds. Following his marriage to Helen, Sir Colin's daughter, John MacGregor of Glenstrae became hereditary captain of Kilchurn. In 1550, 'Grey Colin' granted a lease to 'My beloved servant John MacConoquy MacGregor' (apparently his eldest grandson), that included the tacks of three farms in Glenorchy as well as the grazing on the Quhosche, the land round the castle, for six newly calved milk cows. John paid a rent of 48 bolls of meal, together with an extra 14 bolls for the watermill at nearby Kinchracken. In addition, he had to employ a gardener and provide a clean bed of straw for Sir Colin whenever he visited the castle.

'Grey Colin' was succeeded by his son, Duncan Campbell, 7th of Glenorchy ('Black Duncan of the Cowl') who rebuilt the south-west wing and made extensive alterations *c.*1615.

Sir John Campbell, 10th of Glenorchy, was created Earl of Breadalbane by Charles II in 1681. Although originally a Jacobite, he 'turned his coat' and built the two ranges of barracks on the north side of the castle at the request of King William III in 1690.

The castle was already largely ruinous when seen by William Wordsworth and his sister Dorothy in 1803.

> *Child of loud-throated War! The mountain stream*
> *Roars in thy hearing; but thy hour of rest*
> *Is come, and thou art silent in thy age;*
> *Save when the wind sweeps by and sounds are caught.*

Placed in the care of the then Department of Environment in 1953, the castle was sold by the late Countess of Breadalbane *c.*1986. Today it is owned by local business man, Ian Cleaver, although it is maintained by Historic Scotland, which has carried out extensive restoration to this ancient fortress of Argyll.

Duncan Ladasach

John MacGregor of Glenstrae, who was appointed hereditary custodian of Kilchurn Castle, unfortunately died as a young man in 1528. His second son, Allaster, succeeded him as a minor and the leadership of Clan Gregor was seized by Duncan Ladasach, great grandson of Gregor Aulin.

Duncan, who had possessed a small estate called 'Ardchoille', was now living on Rannoch where he held the castle on the Isle. From here he and his band of caterans raided the surrounding land.

> In the nicht the loud coronach, God wit,
> Was at our tail with monye roustie akes;
> We had the kye, and they got but the glaiks.

Unfortunately, Allaster, the young chief, fell beneath Duncan's thrall. Together, they attacked his mother's people, the Campbells of Glenorchy. Then, more boldly, they raided Strathbraan where they carried off Struan Robertson, chief of the Clan Donnachie.

Allaster, too, died young. His eldest son had been killed by an arrow during a fight, so it was Gregor, known as 'Gregor Roy' for his red hair, who succeeded when he was under age. Duncan Ladasach, who reputedly claimed that he 'lovit never justice nor yet law,' became the tutor, or guardian, of the young man.

Sir Colin Campbell, 6th of Glenorchy ('Grey Colin'), had a particular loathing for Duncan Ladasach. Eventually he captured him (it is said by treachery) and beheaded him, together with two of his sons, in 1552.

Four years later, in 1556, Sir Colin Campbell bought the superiority, or legal control, of the twenty merkland of Glenstrae from Archibald, 6th Earl of Argyll, who also granted him the ward and marriage of Gregor MacGregor, heir of the late Allaster. The MacGregors, therefore, in one swoop, lost not only the protection of their former overlord but also the independence of their chief. Indeed, Sir Colin refused to enfeoff Gregor Roy when he came of age.

Sir Colin even had a hand in his death. The tragic story of which is told in the story of Glen Lyon. Sir Colin Campbell of Glenorchy, 'Grey Colin', obtained a warrant for Gregor MacGregor's arrest.

Pursued and captured, he was executed at Campbell's castle of Balloch, at the foot of Loch Tay, in April 1570. His wife, pregnant with their second child, being forced to witness his death.

Gregor Roy's son, Alasdair, became the young chief, and he and his brother (possibly a posthumous child) grew up at Stronmelochan in Glenstrae. Despite his rank, he did not receive any education, as is proved by a document of 1596 which he signed 'with my hand touching the notary's pen underwritten, because I cannot write'.

Nonetheless, Alasdair had early instruction in the art of swordsmanship, at that time in the Highlands so essential to a man's survival. He also became a skilled archer. An old rhyme describes the bows and arrows of his day:

Bow from yew of Esragin
Eagle feather from Loch Treig,
Yellow wax from Galway town,
And arrow-head made by MacPhedran.[7]

Alasdair, whose mother, remember, was a daughter of Campbell of Glen Lyon, was called the 'Arrow of Glen Lyon'.

Would I could see thee again in the hills of the deer,
With keen-edged spear and hounds in leash, following the chase;
often the king of the forest fell to thy bow of yew –
terror of all our foes, pride of Glenlyon!
Thou wert a skilled fletcher, thy quiver ever full.
See how the sharp arrow is winged with the eagle's plume,
Bound with silken thread, red and green, from Ireland,
Waxed to shield the polished shaft from the heat of the sun.

So sang the bards of Alasdair MacGregor, loud voiced in his praise. Sadly, when he was still a young man, Alasdair was held responsible for the murder of a man named Drummondearnach, head forester in Glen Artney. Any MacGregor known to have a grudge against him was accused of the crime, although there is reason to believe that MacDonalds of Glencoe were the real culprits. The Privy Council declared Alasdair an outlaw, but later, having sworn obedience to James VI, he was actually taken into the royal household for some time.

Not long afterwards, however, Alasdair became the victim of the increasing rivalry between the chiefs of the Campbells – Archibald, 7th Earl of Argyll, and Sir Duncan Campbell of Glenorchy. Two MacGregors had slaughtered and eaten 'a black wedder with a white tail' on land belonging to Colquhoun of Luss. They were killed by Colquhoun's men and the MacGregors plotted revenge.

Argyll, who had quarrelled with Colquhoun, was aware of this and is said to have incited Alasdair to take action against him. A battle took place in Glen Fruin and many on both sides, including some innocent spectators, were killed. The Colquhoun women reputedly carried their men's bloodstained shirts to the king, and James, who detested the sight of such gore, ordered Alasdair's arrest.

Alasdair's grandmother was a daughter of Campbell of Ardkinglas. Now her people betrayed him and took him prisoner. They forced him into a boat to sail down Loch Fyne to Inveraray and the prison of Argyll. It was January and ice skimmed the surface of the water but Alasdair leapt overboard and somehow swam to the shore.

He then surrendered to Argyll on the Earl's promise that he would see him safely over the Border into England. Argyll was as good as his word, but once across the Border Alasdair was again arrested and taken back to Edinburgh in chains. Imprisoned, he was tried, convicted of treason and sentenced to die. One small concession was granted. He was hanged as befitted a chief at double his own height, above another four men of his clan, in April 1604.

Brutal punishment was then inflicted upon the clan MacGregor as a whole. The name was proscribed by an Act of Parliament, only rescinded in 1775. The wearing of their tartan was forbidden. Anyone could legally shoot a MacGregor and were rewarded for doing so. The men were butchered and the women branded with a hot iron. Some fled from Glenstrae on to the Moor of Rannoch where they lived, largely by stealing cattle, in any way they could.

They burned Sir Duncan Campbell's newly built castle of Achallader and then, most probably in darkness, descended on Kilchurn where they killed his most prized possession, the stallion which had been a present from Prince Henry (son of Charles I) together with forty great mares.

Desperate men as they were, with such actions they certainly sealed their own fate. Sir Duncan gathered a large force and, in the summer of 1610, destroyed every building that the MacGregors possessed in Glenstrae. Not a stone was left of the old fortalice of Stronmelochan. Flaming torches of pine-wood, tipped with tar, were thrust below the thatch of every cottage and barn. Likewise, the crops were ruined, the grain stolen, and every animal either killed or driven away.

Thus, the people of Clan Gregor, driven into the remotest parts of the mountains as outlaws, became known throughout the Highlands as the 'Children of the Mist'.

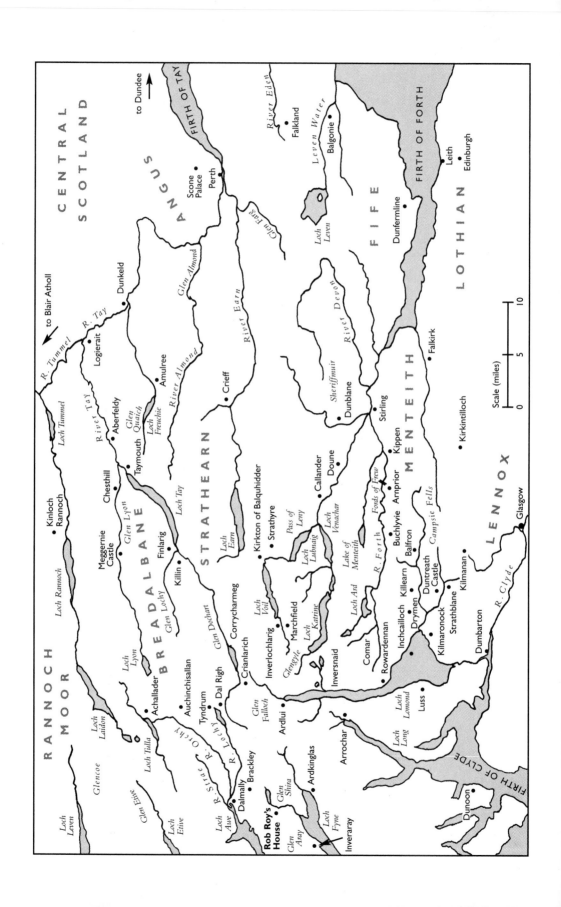

CHAPTER II

Training of a Warrior

Boyhood in Glengyle

Glengyle, the upper end of Strath Gartney, is one of the wildest places in Scotland. The name derives from *Gleann Goill*, meaning the 'forked glen'. No road traverses it. Only a row of electricity pylons indicate the present age. The River Gyle rises as a burn on the east side of the watershed of the mountain range above Loch Lomond. A rough path from Parlan Hill at its source leads west into Glen Falloch, while to the east a burn winds its way to Loch Doine in Balquhidder. The land on both sides of this range of hills, crowned by the mighty peak of Ben Lomond, was once MacGregor land.

Today, Glengyle can be reached from the Dukes Road, which crosses the Trossachs. The Victorian passenger steamer, *Sir Walter Scott*, sails the length of Loch Katrine to the foot of the glen, which can also be reached by a track along the loch shore. In Rob Roy's time, however, the glen was a barely accessible rock-bound stronghold where men could hide in safety from authority. To enter without permission or substantial protection would be to take your life in your hands. Travellers from the Lowlands did not go unarmed or alone.

The River Gyle from its source is joined by other burns which, in spate, plunge like waving tails of white horses from the steep hills on either side. On calm days, the main stream runs smoothly; pools, amber in sunlight, are shadowed blue-grey under cloud. The high tops of the mountains above are remote even today. In the seventeenth century, they were the haunt of foxes and even a few wolves.

Gradually, the glen widens before it enters Loch Katrine, the main water supply for Glasgow since 1859. Because of the necessity to maintain its level, the loch was dammed with the result that some of the land at the mouth of Glengyle is now under water.

Glengyle House, of nineteenth-century date, now belongs to the Glasgow Water Board. It is believed to stand close to the site of the house where, in 1671, Rob Roy MacGregor was born.

Rob Roy's father, Lieutenant-Colonel MacGregor, or *Donald Glas* ('Grey Donald') as he was known, was chief of *Clan Dugal Ciar*, the cadet branch of Clan Gregor which descends from Dugal Ciar.[8] His mother, Margaret, was a grand-daughter of Duncan Roy Campbell of Glen Lyon. Robert, as he was christened, was the youngest of their three sons. The eldest was Iain (Gaelic for 'John'), the second Duncan, and their only daughter was given her mother's name.

The original Glengyle House would, in all likelihood, have been a typical laird's dwelling of the time. Architectural plans of similar buildings show two, if not three, floors. The roof may have been thatched, slates being expensive and hard to obtain, but chimney stacks would have been built within the gable walls.

The people who lived in the low dry-stone cottages of the farming townships, of which few traces now remain, were Donald's sub-tenants who worked for him part-time in return for a patch of ground on which they kept their animals, including the all important cows. In summer they drove his cattle to the hill with their own and herded them on the *airidhs*, or upper pastures, to keep them off the low ground where corn, kale and some hay were grown.

Rob Roy, as he grew older, worked at the busy times. It was now that he acquired the good eye for cattle for which he was afterwards famed. More importantly, as the chief's son, he learned the use of weapons and was taught the rudiments of battle drill so that in times of emergency he could both lead and deploy men in war.

As soon as they were able, boys were taught sword drill. They practised with sticks at first and only when they were strong enough to handle them could proper weapons be used. A basket-handled sword was easier to manipulate than the massive two-handed claymore, which could sweep a man's head from his shoulders when powered by the strength of both arms.

Rob Roy proved a natural swordsman. Although not very tall – he was slightly above average in height – he had excessively broad shoulders and legs which have been described as like those of a Highland bull. Most importantly he had long arms. The story that he could tie his garters without bending down may be an exaggeration, but he certainly did have the most important asset of a swordsman, that of a very long reach.

He wore the Highland dress of kilt and plaid. The latter, thrown over his shoulder for walking, became a blanket at night. The wool, when wet, contained the body's heat and heather made a good enough bed. Highland people went barefoot in the summer but Colonel Donald and his sons probably had leather boots, made by a local shoemaker, for the winter months.[9]

Like all boys in the Highlands, Rob Roy became hardened to physical strain. It was nothing for a man to walk fifty miles or so, covering the distance with a loping stride. Although as a young man he had not yet reached his full strength he had already acquired the fitness for which he was later so renowned. With leg muscles like iron, he could travel for miles over the hills, sleeping at night wrapped in his plaid. As was the custom, he would have a bag of meal tied to his belt; this meal, when mixed with water, could keep him going for days.

Donald Glas was among the first of the Highland chiefs to organise a form of protection called a 'Watch', an enterprise evolving from the constant theft of cattle at that time. By the terms of their agreement, he and those involved agreed, for a fee, to ensure the safety of other clansmen's cattle, both on the lands of their owners and when being driven to the markets. Donald's sons are known to have gone with him on his journeys to make arrangements for the safe transport of cattle and to receive the payment or 'mail' – from which derives the word 'blackmail' – that was due.

In those days a Highlander's most prized possession was invariably his gun. A flintlock, also called a 'hagbut' or an 'arquebus', was largely used for shooting birds, but the long-barrelled gun, imported from Spain and often called the *t-slinneanach* in Gaelic, with its greater range, was the best for killing deer.

The people of the Highlands depended largely on salted down venison to survive the winter months. Deer drives took place in the autumn when the beasts were chased from the high tops by men with dogs and driven into an enclosed place, such as a narrow ravine, where they could be shot. Cruel as this sounds, a cull of some sort was necessary as families might otherwise have starved.

Unlike the great majority of people in Scotland at that time Rob Roy and his brothers, as the sons of a chief, were taught to read and write. Gaelic was their first language but they also became literate in the English tongue. Their sister had no education other than that of learning household skills. It was thought unnecessary and in fact dangerous in those times for women to be able to communicate through the written word. The boys were probably tutored by the minister as few schools existed except in the larger villages and towns. The fact of Rob Roy possessing both a good vocabulary and a fair way of expression is proved by his letters of later years.

At home, he would have had access to his father's precious books, in particular the Bible, which in a Highland house took pride of place. The MacGregors of Glengyle lived within the Parish of Callander where it was recorded that Robert MacGregor was christened on 7 March 1671, within a few days of his birth.

The MacGregors, like many of the Highland clans, belonged to the Scottish Episcopal Church. Rob Roy grew up using the old prayer book established by James VI & I. Later in life, however, he was to convert to the Roman Catholic faith.

Controversy over religion dominated the politics of the times. The Jacobites, as those loyal to James VII & II came to be called, were in the main part Catholics or Episcopalians, while those who supported William III were mostly Presbyterians. Broadly speaking, the Highlands, with the notable exception of Argyll, were for the Stewart King James, while the Lowlands, dominated by Whig lairds, were largely for the Dutch William.

Rock pool on the River Gyle

Rannoch Moor with Glencoe in the distance

The Sow of Atholl and An Torc at Drumochter Pass

The River Garry, near Killiecrankie, flanked by autumn trees

CHAPTER III

The Rising of 1689

Prelude to War

Rob Roy was seventeen years old when, on 10 June, 1688, James Prince of Wales (destined to become known as the 'Old Pretender') was born. Shortly afterwards, news reached England that William, Prince of Orange and husband of the king's Protestant daughter Mary, intended to invade and, on behalf of the Protestant people of England, to claim the throne.

King James, greatly alarmed at this threat from his son-in-law, ordered the Privy Council of Scotland to send an army to his aid. The force which left early in October consisted of two divisions, one of Foot under General Douglas, and the second of Horse under Major-General John Graham of Claverhouse, who was created Viscount Dundee by the king on 10 November. Five days earlier, William of Orange had landed at Torbay in Devon. Many officers of the Royal army deserted to him and King James, loosing his nerve, fled to France to join his wife and child at St Germains on 28 December of that fateful year of 1688. Thus, the 'Glorious Revolution' was won.

In March 1689, the government of Scotland changed as the old Privy Council was replaced by the Convention of Estates. Viscount Dundee, 'having received warning of an attempt to murder him', left the Convention suddenly and was believed to have headed for Dundee. Instead, he managed to climb up the rock and gain entrance to Edinburgh Castle, held by the Duke of Gordon in the name of King James.

The two conferred on the possibilities of a rising to restore the now exiled monarch. There was much support for him in Scotland, particularly among the Catholics and Episcopalians who were resentful of the authority of the re-established Presbyterian Church. Sir Ewan

Cameron of Lochiel, loyal both to the exiled sovereign and to his Episcopalian faith, was known to be forming a conspiracy among the clans of the North West Highlands and the Isles to restore King James.

With this knowledge, Dundee returned to the town of his name to raise his standard in defiance of the Dutch invader who had seized the crown.

Commission to the Laird of MacGregor

In March 1689, King James VII & II landed in Ireland to fight in what developed into a religious war. Believing that his cause might be won in Scotland, he urged the Highland chiefs to rise.

On 17 May, from his court in Dublin Castle, he issued a commission to 'the Laird of MacGregor':

> your Loyalty Courage and Conduct doe by these presents Constitute and appoint you to be Colonell of a Regiment of Foot of our ancient kingdom of Scotland hereby giving you power to name and appoint your Lieut. Colonell, Major, Captains, Lieutenants and Ensigns in your said Regiment.[10]

Gregor MacGregor, chief of Clan Gregor, an only son and unmarried, was living on his estate at Craigrostan on Loch Lomond. He may have been physically or mentally ill for he died only four years later in 1693, aged only thirty-two. Perhaps it was such ill-health that, in 1689, prevented him from taking the field and led him to appoint his relation, Lieutenant Colonel Donald MacGregor of Glengyle, to deputise for him in obeying King James's call to arms.

Donald MacGregor of Glengyle duly accepted King James's commission to raise a regiment and made ready for war. It was now known that General Hugh Mackay of Scourie, who had fought both in Holland and in England for King William, was already in Scotland preparing to subdue his enemies.

Viscount Dundee, in command of the Jacobite army, issued a summons for the clans to assemble at Dalmucomer – a flat stretch of land round the confluence of the River Lochy and the River Spean in the Great Glen – before the middle of May.

The clan Gregor appear to have joined him early in his campaign. From Glengyle, their quickest route would have been into Glen Falloch and from there by way of Crianlarich and Tyndrum and across Rannoch Moor to Glencoe. A short-cut over the 'Devil's' Staircase' would have brought them to the head of Loch Leven, and from there they would have continued past Maryburgh (the old name for Fort William) to reach the Great Glen. The distance they covered cannot have been less than sixty miles. The *Grameid* is an heroic poem by the standard-bearer of Dundee and describes his campaign in 1689; translated from Latin, it reads:

> After this, stalwart Glendessary, Cameron, with his company advances over the plain and with applauding shouts he unfurls mid his Clansmen his ruddy banner, with ancestral rite. Him the tribes of Lonach (the Lennox tribe) and the widely spread clan of McGregor accompanied as their leader.

Among 'the widely spread clan of MacGregor' was the youngest son of Glengyle, the red-haired Robert, now a lad of eighteen. In his bonnet, he wore a sprig of Scots fir, recognisable in a scrimmage as the badge of his clan. In his right hand, he grasped the claymore which he now knew expertly how to handle. His fingers flexed in readiness on the hilt. This, at last, was real war.

The MacGregor contingent, not large enough to form a regiment, was joined to the Camerons of Glendessary.[11] Now, for the first time, Rob Roy set eyes on the great Highland chiefs, who already were legends in their time. Sir Ewan Cameron of Lochiel, he who had bitten the throat out of an enemy; and the still, upright figure of a white-haired man of nearly eighty – none other than MacIain of Glencoe.

From Dalmucomer, the Jacobite army headed south over the Drumochter Pass. With pipes skirling and banners flying, Dundee led his army through Glen Spean into Badenoch where 'they had useful skirmishing for a month'.[12] Then he temporarily disengaged the men while he waited for MacKay to appear.

From there, it was over the Drumochter Pass and southwards. They assembled again on the 25 July and now it was known that Mackay was north of Perth. On word of this, Dundee marched his force to Blair Castle where, without meeting opposition, he encamped. The sons of the Duke Atholl, as so often occurs in civil wars, had adhered to opposite sides. Lord Murray, the Duke's eldest son, held the castle with a small garrison for the government but, knowing his force would be inadequate against the approaching host, he now hastily withdrew.

Dundee arrived at the castle on the evening of Friday, 26 July. Next morning, news reached him that Mackay was at Moulin, above Pitlochry; the astute Jacobite commander lost no time in skilfully deploying his men.

The Pass of Killiecrankie

The River Garry, which flows in a broad stream below Blair Castle, narrows into a steep gorge, called the 'Pass of Killiecrankie', before it converges with the River Tummel just above Pitlochry.

Today, the A9 runs above the Pass and is one of the busiest roads in Scotland. Driving along in a car, it is difficult to realise that three hundred years ago, going either north or south, one would have been forced to inch one's way along the narrow track which followed the precipitous slope on the east side of the Pass.

On Saturday, 27 July 1689, the soldiers commanded by General MacKay, weighed down by their new bayonets, scrambling and slipping in the heat, cursed the fate that had brought them to this accursed track through a cleft. Sometimes, looking below, they gasped with terror at the thought of plunging to their deaths. Then, grasping their weapons more tightly, they steeled themselves against what lay ahead.

Dundee, who had led his men behind the Hill of Lude, had stationed them on Craigellachie Hill above the low ridge where now stands the House of Urrard. Below lay the River Garry and its adjacent meadow land, on to which the enemy must emerge from the bottleneck of the Pass.

The MacGregors and the Camerons were in the centre of the army, together with the MacDonalds of Glencoe. The MacLeans, the

MacDonells of Glengarry and the MacDonalds of Clanranald were on the right and the MacDonalds of Sleat on the left.

The Highlanders waited impatiently, gripping their axes and claymores, longing to get at the foe. They saw the red-coated soldiers string out below them as Mackay made the fatal mistake of over-extending his line. But the sun was in their eyes and it was not until eight in the evening, as the last rays of light disappeared behind the hills, that Dundee gave the order to charge.

Sir Ewan Cameron of Lochiel, a man of sixty, threw off his boots and ran barefoot ahead of his men. Many clansmen were killed or wounded by initial gunfire, but the soldiers were still fumbling with their unfamiliar bayonets, trying to screw them into the muzzle of their guns, as the screaming horde fell upon them with claymores and the fearful Lochaber axes that could split a skull apart.

The Pass behind the soldiers became a scene of horror as men, in a state of panic, fell and were trampled upon by others trying to force their way back. Some, loosing their footing, fell into the river and many drowned. It is claimed that in the space of five minutes two thousand soldiers died.

Dundee, aware he had won a great victory, dismounted behind the House of Urrard to let his horse drink at a well. The light was now dim, but a sniper within the house recognised the tall figure and, through an open window, killed him with a shot through the eye.

Legend has it that when he heard what had occurred, King William said that there was now no danger of revolution because Dundee was dead.

Dunkeld

The ancient town of Dunkeld beside the River Tay in the centre of Scotland was the capital of Kenneth MacAlpin (Kenneth I) who became king in 843. He founded or enlarged the cathedral to hold the relics of St Columba, the saint associated with the monastery which formerly stood on the site.

In August 1689, following the victory of Killiecrankie, the Jacobite army, now commanded by Colonel Cannon who had replaced the gallant Dundee, attacked the town. Lieut-Colonel Donald MacGregor of Glengyle led his contingent of kilted men scrambling over the walls. His second son Duncan was taken prisoner during street fighting which lasted for four hours.

The Highlanders confronted the Cameronians, a regiment just formed by the Earl of Angus from devout Covenanting men. Fighting with desperate bravery, even after their young commander, Colonel Cleland, was killed, they ran short of ammunition but made bullets from lead, which they stripped from the roof of the Duke of Atholl's house. Colonel Cannon, a man without Dundee's power of leadership, believed the day to be lost and ordered the buglers to sound a retreat.

—

Following the battle much of the town was rebuilt. The cathedral, already unroofed following the Reformation, was among the buildings restored.

The thirteenth-century choir is now the parish church. Since the Second World War much work has been carried out in Dunkeld by the National Trust.

Blair Castle

Standing as it does below heather-covered hills, the white-washed Blair Castle retains its medieval splendour to the present day. Built originally in 1263 by the Comyns on land owned by David Strathbogie, Earl of Atholl, the castle later passed to the Stewart Earls of Atholl. Then, in 1629, it was granted to John Murray, Master of Tullibardine.

Sixty years later, in 1689, the Marquis of Tullibardine, eldest son of the Duke of Atholl and his brother, Lord George Murray, the Duke's third son, were loyal to the exiled James VII & II. The king was at that time in Ireland, where the mostly Catholic people supported him, and there were hopes that the king of France would send an army to his aid.

On 24 August, Lord George Murray summoned the Jacobite chiefs to Blair Castle. Among them was Lieutenant-Colonel Donald MacGregor of Glengyle, who (acting for his chief), signed a Bond of Association by which he committed himself to meeting again in September with no less than a hundred men.

——

Prince Charles Edward stayed at Blair Castle on his march to Edinburgh in 1745, Later, held by a Hanoverian garrison, it was actually attacked and damaged by Lord George Murray, commander of the army of the Prince.

It was rebuilt by Lord George's older brother, the 2nd Duke, during the eighteenth century. Then, in 1872, the 7th Duke employed the architect David Bryce to restore it to the look of the original castle.

Glen Lyon

Glen Lyon, the longest glen in Scotland, stretches for thirty miles. It is a place of great antiquity, long inhabited by man. The yew tree by the church at Fortingall, in the mouth of the glen, is said to have been planted by Pontius Pilate and may be two thousand years old.

Upstream from Fortingall, the road follows the River Lyon through the Pass of Chesthill before reaching the floor of the glen. Mountains tower up on either side. It can be likened to a fastness of the Gods. In pre-historic times, a chain of round towers still called *Caistealan nam Fiann* ('castles of the Fingalians'), now long vanished, stretched along the whole length of the glen.

Later, in early Christian times (*c*.560 AD) St Eonan, a disciple of St Columba, settled in the glen. He is said to have saved people from a plague by telling them to leave their contaminated houses and go to the hills. The rock on which he preached, called *Craig-dianaidh* ('rock of safety'), remained a place of conference for many years.

Glen Lyon, according to legend, was held first by seven successive chiefs of the MacGregors. The MacGregors of Roro continued to live there, as vassals of the Campbells, after Clan Gregor had been proscribed. Later, seven Campbell chiefs of a cadet branch of the Campbells of Glenorchy held the glen. Here it was that the unfortunate Gregor Roy, chief of the MacGregors of Glenstrae, was hunted to his death by Sir Colin Campbell ('Grey Colin'), 6th of Glenorchy, in 1570.

According to the Glen Lyon lore, Duncan Campbell of Glen Lyon, who lived at Carnban or *Caisteal a Curin-Bhan* ('Castle of the White Cairn'), which is about two miles above the Pass of Chesthill, had a daughter whom he intended giving in marriage to the Baron of Dall, on the south side of Loch Tay. However, his 'daughter was of a different opinion for, having met with young Gregor MacGregor of Glenstrae, she gave up to him her heart's warmest affections and which he fully returned. In spite of all opposition she left her father's house and married him . . . In consequence, Gregor and his wife were followed with the most unrelenting enmity.'

Gregor's young wife did return to the shelter of her father's house – perhaps to give birth to her son – and Gregor visited her secretly at night. During one assignation, he was betrayed and in running for his life, jumped the River Lyon at a place still called 'MacGregor's Leap'. Their love story is part of Glen Lyon tradition and continues:

> They were often obliged to wander from place to place, taking shelter in caves under rocks and in thickets of woods. On the night preceding 5 April, 1570, they had rested under a rock on a hillside above Loch Tay. Next morning after taking such breakfast as in the circumstance they could compass, the young wife sat herself on the ground, and dandled her young babe in her arms whilst Gregor was fondly playing with it . . . In an instant, they were surrounded by a band of their foes and carried off to Balloch. Gregor was at once condemned to death and beheaded at Kenmore in the presence of Sir Colin.

Some accounts say that Sir Colin or his son Duncan (notorious, like his father, for his persecution of the MacGregors), actually wielded the axe, watched by various neighbours, including the Earl of Atholl, the Lord Justice Clerk and Gregor's father-in-law, Duncan Campbell of Glen Lyon.

The traditional tale ends: 'Most pitiful of all, the unutterably wretched wife was forced to witness her husband's execution.

Immediately thereafter, with her babe in her arms, she was driven forth by her kindred, helpless and houseless.'[13] The kindness, however, thus cruelly denied was abundantly given by others who pitied her sad case. In her great anguish, she composed the Gaelic song *Cumha Ghriogair mhicGhriogair* ('Lament for Gregor MacGregor') which begins:

Ochan, ochan, ochan, uirigh,
'S goirt mo chridhe a laoigh;
Ochan, achan, ochani uirigh,
Cha chluinn d'athair ar caoidh.

Ochan, ochan, ochan, ooree,
Breaks my heart my own wee dear,
Ochan, ochan, ochan ooree,
Thy slain father cannot hear.

The boy to whom she reputedly sang this lullaby (the real author is unknown) was Alasdair, her son, who was himself executed in 1604.

The ruins of the Campbell's first castle, called 'Carnban', stand on a conical hill about three miles beyond the entrance to the glen. A later laird, known as 'Mad Colin', who married a sister of the notorious Sir Duncan Campbell, 7th of Glenorchy, built Meggernie Castle near its head.

Sir Robert Campbell, 9th of Glenorchy (*d*. 1657), had a daughter Jean, who married Archibald, the son of Duncan Roy Campbell, 4th of Glen Lyon. Their son, Robert, became the 5th chief of Glen Lyon. They also had two daughters: Margaret, who married Donald Glas of Glengyle in 1656 and thereby became the mother of Rob Roy, and Mary, who married Malcolm MacGregor, 8th of Glenstrae, then chief of Clan Gregor, although no longer in possession of Glenstrae.

Robert Campbell of Glen Lyon, born in 1632, was an exceptionally handsome young man. He largely rebuilt Meggernie Castle where, renowned for his extravagance, he entertained in style. Running short of money, however, he was forced to sell his estate of Glen Lyon to Lord Murray in 1684.

Raid of Glen Lyon

The people of Glen Lyon were still harvesting when the MacDonalds, who had fought at Killiecrankie, headed homewards through Glen Lyon. Foremost among them were their fearsome chiefs, MacDonald of Keppoch or 'Coll of the Cows' as he was known, and old MacIain of Glencoe.

The MacDonalds fell upon the little farming towns in Glen Lyon, stripping them like foxes chewing to the marrow of the bone. Everything that could be driven or carried off was seized . . . a baby wrapped in a rug was lifted, the rug whipped off and the infant left naked on the floor.

The money value of all that was taken in the glen – 36 horses, 240 cows, 993 sheep, 133 goats and the contents of houses down to the glass in the windows – amounted to £7,540, 17s, 11d Scots. Robert Campbell, who now lived off his wife's small estate of Chesthill, lost property worth about £3,000. Almost penniless, he was driven to live by his sword and in 1690, at the age of fifty-seven, he obtained the command of a company in the Earl of Argyll's Regiment of Foot.

Two years later, in 1692, he was acting under orders when sent to subdue the men who had partly ruined him, the MacDonalds of Glencoe.

Meggernie Castle

Meggernie Castle was originally designed as a fortress to command the head of Glen Lyon. Some of the walls are pierced with shot-holes through which muskets were fired. Built by 'Mad Colin' Campbell, laird of Glen Lyon in about 1585 as a tower house of four storeys and an attic, it was altered and enlarged by his descendant, Robert Campbell, 5th of Glen Lyon, in the later half of the sixteenth century.

When he became bankrupt in 1684, the castle was sold to Lord Murray, later the Duke of Atholl, and was subsequently bought by

James Menzies of Culdares. The castle is said to be haunted by the ghost of the beautiful wife of one of the Menzies lairds, who, believing her to be unfaithful, murdered her and cut her body in two. The bones of the upper half of a skeleton, found by workmen, were reburied, but the ghost reputedly remains.

Later the castle belonged to the Stewarts of Cardney who held it until 1885.

Additions to the original tower-house include a ballroom which was added by the Wills family during the 1960s. The present owner is Beverley Malin. The whole castle, now white-washed, stands as though still in protection of the upper reaches of Glen Lyon.

Arrest and Imprisonment of Donald MacGregor of Glengyle

Following the defeat of the Jacobite army at Dunkeld in August 1689, the MacDonalds were not the only people to seize the chance of taking cattle from the enemies of King James.

William Cochrane of Kilmaronock, a laird with an estate in the valley of the Endrick, which flows into the south-east end of Loch Lomond, refused to pay his annual fee for the Watch to Rob Roy's father, Donald Glas. The sixteen bolls of meal, worth about £80 in Scots money, to which Donald was due were of vital necessity to the survival, not only of his own family, but of many others in Glengyle during the coming winter months.

Cochrane repeatedly turned a deaf ear to demands for payment and Donald Glas, infuriated, decided to take cows in lieu of grain.

Somehow Cochrane was warned and a company of Lord Kenmure's regiment from Drymen barracks hid in waiting among trees. Donald was seized and taken prisoner as he and his gillies were actually driving a herd away.

Held first in Stirling Castle, he was later conveyed to the Tolbooth, the common prison in Edinburgh, where his second son Duncan had been kept in close confinement since being captured in August at Dunkeld. The conditions of the jail were so filthy and the food so inadequate that both father and son never fully recovered from the privations they endured.

Duncan was released in the following March of 1690, but his father was held prisoner until October 1691.

CHAPTER IV

The Glengyle Watch

To Catch a Thief . . .

Lieutenant-Colonel Donald MacGregor was still a prisoner in the Tolbooth in Edinburgh during the autumn of 1691 when he heard to his great sorrow that his wife Margaret had died. William Cochrane of Kilmaronock, whose cattle he had been lifting when taken prisoner, surprisingly refused to charge him and in February the Keeper of the Edinburgh Tolbooth was instructed by the Lords of the Privy Council to set Lieutenant-Colonel Donald MacGregor free. The conditions attached to his being given his liberty included that 'he and Robert and John (Iain) MacGregor, his sons . . . shall live peaceably and with all submission to the present Government . . . and shall not intercommune, converse or correspond with any rebels.'[14]

Donald of Glengyle was now a sick man. Fifteen years later, Doctor George Stirling was still demanding payment from the government for money due to his father 'for attendance upon and furnishing medicines to the prisoners of the Government . . . such as Colonel MacGregor and his servants'. Donald was also charged for his keep in prison, at the rate of sixpence a day, and non-payment would seem to account for his not being released until the following October, having then been held for two years.

During his father's absence the organisation of his cattle protection business fell upon Iain, his eldest son. Donald Glas, when he agreed to raise a company for King James, had taken the wise precaution of leaving Iain at home, ostensibly to look after the farm. Thus, he was not a rebel, according to the law.

Lord Breadalbane, the main adviser to the government on Highland matters, promoted the idea of 'Watches' as a means of ensuring that cattle reached the markets in safety. Discontented Highland Jacobites, following the Revolution, increasingly regarded the herds of the Whig Lowland lairds as fair game. The MacGregors of Glengyle were Jacobites but none had a better knowledge of the cattle business, legal or otherwise, than they. Breadalbane, himself described as 'wily as a fox', was prepared to 'set a thief to catch a thief', as the old saying goes.

So, upon his suggestion, the Privy Council, on 12 February 1691, decreed that 'Upon the petition of William Cochrane of Kilmaronock, and eleven others . . . gentlemen heritors in the westend of the Sheriffdom of Stirling, and within the shire of Dumbarton lying on the braes of the Highlands,' John (Iain) MacGregor of Glengyle and Archibald MacGregor of Kilmanan were appointed to the joint command of a Highland Watch.[15]

Two months later, in April, Breadalbane put his idea to the test when a party of MacRaes from Kintail descended on his own land at Finlarig and stole fifteen of his cows. Incensed, he despatched a runner to Glengyle to summon Rob Roy, who set off, with twelve of his own men, to find the beasts and bring them home.

Anyone who has ever dragged in a deer knows that grass, and particularly heather, lies flattened for several days after being tramped down. So it was easy to follow the trail from Finlarig, across Rannoch Moor and through the Forest of Mamlorn. Thereafter, however, it became more difficult on the harder, steeper ground and the signs disappeared completely somewhere beyond Glen Spean. The men were beginning to grumble – they had now covered nearly seventy miles over largely trackless ground. This was a wild goose chase; they wanted to go home. But Rob Roy, in no uncertain manner, forced them on . . .

They found themselves in the deep and narrow glen of one of the burns which run from the height of Cairn Dearg into the top of Glen Roy, near the headwaters of the Spey. A glimmer of light ahead proved to be a tinkers' fire. From them the hunters discovered that a party of men with cattle were in a corrie higher up the burn.

Scrambling upwards, moving silently over the hill in the dusk, they found the MacRaes preparing to drive the cattle stealthily through the night. With a yell, they fell upon the thieves, swinging their vicious claymores. Cattle bellowed in terror as men lunged at each other across their backs. Rob Roy is said to have been wounded and nearly killed by the leader of the MacRaes, but managed to duck beneath his guard and stab him to death with his dirk.

He returned in triumph to Finlarig where Breadalbane paid him. More importantly, however, the word soon spread around that young MacGregor, he with the red hair, was the man you needed to get your cattle back. There was business for the Glengyle Watch.

Finlarig Castle

This stronghold of Breadalbane was built in the 1620s by his ancestor Sir Duncan Campbell, 7th of Glenorchy, known both as 'Duncan of the Castles' and 'Black Duncan of the Cowl'. Today, only two ruined towers and the vestiges of a kitchen are all that remain of this once formidable tower house which stood guard over the west end of Loch Tay.

Now it is a peaceful place where birds nest undisturbed in the ivy that climbs over the walls, but near to the castle the beheading pit indicates the turbulent past. Within it a hollowed-out stone supported many a noble neck as the axe fell in execution. The more ordinary people were hanged from a tree outside. In Rob Roy's time a dangling corpse was used to deter criminals much as a crow hanging from a gibbet frightens off marauding birds. The rights of a barony, including that of pit and gallows, remained until hereditary jurisdiction was ended by an Act of Parliament following the Jacobite Rising of 1745.

The Hership of Kippen

The summer of 1691 passed and Donald Glas, now very ill and frail, was still in the Edinburgh Tolbooth. Officially, he had been released in February but was being held until his prison debts were re-paid. His rents from his tenants are said to have been seized by soldiers and it seems that it was the desperate need for money, needed to secure his father's freedom, that prompted Donald's youngest son to purloin some cattle for himself. The legend, handed down for three hundred years, has certainly a ring of truth.

The story goes that Sir Alexander Livingstone of Bedlormie, a large landowner in Stirlingshire, was a turncoat with a great deal to answer for. Therefore, when it became known that a big herd of cattle, which he had bought at Dumbarton, was being driven towards Stirling along the old road that runs below the Gargunnock Hills, the chance seemed too good to miss.

With a band of his men, Rob Roy went to Buchlyvie. They found the little village almost deserted, the people harvesting in the fields. In the evening, as everyone returned, Rob Roy and his men moved out of the village and on to the Kippen Muir. But the villagers pursued them, threatening them with scythes, pitchforks and cudgels. Other men from the neighbouring villages of Kippen and Balfron appeared to give support. Stones and turfs began to fly and the MacGregors were about to withdraw when, in the west, a herd of two hundred cattle blocked out the setting sun.

Swords now drawn, Rob Roy and his men easily captured the beasts. The villagers scattered and it is claimed that in passing through Kippen the MacGregors took a cow from every byre. Shortly, they reached the Forth and it was here, at the Fords of Frew, that the last act of the drama occurred. The cattle were nearly across when a party of dragoons from Cardross came galloping upon the scene. A trooper, raising his sword, crashed it upon Rob Roy's head. 'Damn ye, your mother never wrought your night-cap!' he yelled as his weapon clanged on the iron plate in MacGregor's bonnet. Stunned, Rob Roy fell upon his knees. From the corner of his eye he saw the soldier raise his arm again but in the same second he recognised the huge figure of a man called Macanleister raising a musket to his shoulder.

'Och, Macanleister, is there nothing in her?' he somehow managed to croak as, in the same instant, there came a shattering report and the dragoon fell on top of him, sliding dead from his horse.

Thus runs the story, no doubt embellished over the years. More factually, the records of the Privy Council of Scotland, for 1 October 1691, state tellingly that 'Col. MacGregor – takes the oath of allegiance – any little means he had, spent – his wife lately died, be liberated without payment of house or servants dues'.[16]

Glen Lyon hills in winter

Ruins of Finlarig, near Killin

Rock on Beinn Chaorach in the Forest of Mamlorn

Sunrise over Loch Arklet

Glencoe

Glencoe has a sinister atmosphere even on a sunlit day. The massive peaks, rising from the glen on either side, seem to draw in around as though hiding it from the sun. *Bidean nam Bian*, to the south of the glen, at 3,766 feet, is the highest peak in Argyll, *Stob Coire an Lochain* is 3,675 feet in height and *Beinn Fhadda* (the 'Long Hill') rises 3,500 feet above sea level.

Glencoe was the hunting ground of the heroes of Ossian, about whom the Gaelic poems, handed down by word of mouth through generations, were recited round the peat fires. Ossian's cave can be seen high up on Aonach Dubh, and further down the glen, on the east side of the river, rises *Sgùrr nan Féinne*, hill of the legendary warriors who came from Ireland to help the people of Scotland drive invading Norsemen from their shores.

Today, the land round the bed of the river holds a few sheep and cows, but at one time every little scrap of ground that could be turned over with a plough or a spade was cultivated, as traces of furrows prove. The glen was then loud with the lowing of cattle, for it is reckoned that in the late 1600s it held about a thousand cows.

Some belonged to the people who farmed in the many little townships in Glencoe and the adjoining glens, but many had been 'lifted' from neighbours who searched for them without success. The MacDonalds were experts at taking cattle, usually on moonlit nights. They also were adept at hiding them in well-guarded secluded corries which few could ever find. It is said that:

> Once in Glencoe it was impossible to recover the prey. Let any number be sent against them, his [Maclain's] gillies guarded the narrow passes; at the preconcerted signal the cattle and people removed to the rocky fastnesses which a few men could hold against an army. The foe had nothing to wreck his vengeance upon but a few turf-built huts, as easily rebuilt as they were cast down.[17]

Many of the people in the little farming townships were saved by their knowledge of the escape routes on high ground on one dreadful snowbound night of 13 February 1692.

Those who carried out the 'Massacre of Glencoe' on the orders of

King William III cannot be exonerated, but the king himself and the Secretary of State, the Master of Stair, must take most of the blame. The Earl of Breadalbane, master of double-dealing, was also to some extent involved.

Captain Robert Campbell of Glen Lyon received the instructions in a letter from Lieutenant-Colonel James Hamilton, Deputy-Governor of Fort William, to the officer stationed at Ballachulish, who sent it on, containing the following words:

> Sir,
>
> Persuand to the commander in chief's and my Colonel's orders to me for putting in execution the service commanded against the rebels in Glencoe, wherein yow, with the party of the Earl of Argyle's regiment under your command, are to be concerned, yow are therefore forthwith to order your affairs, so that the several posts already assigned by yow be, by yow and your several detachments, fallen in action with precisely, by five o'clock tomorrow morning, being Saturday; at which time I will endeavour the same with those appointed from this regiment for the other places.
>
> It will be most necessary that yow secure the avenues to the south, that the old fox, nor none of his cubs, may gett away. The orders are that none be spared from 70 of the sword, nor the Government troubled with prisoners.
>
> This all until I see you, from
> Your humble servant
> James Hamilton
>
> P. S. Please order a guard to secure the Ferry and the boats there, and the boats must be all on this syde the Ferry after your men are over. [18]

The order was explicit and, despite its brutality, Robert Campbell of Glen Lyon, an army officer who had sworn loyalty to the king, would have faced court-martial and execution had he refused to obey the instructions detailed. Although doubtless glad to get his own back on the MacDonalds who, less than three years before, had ravaged his glen and taken everything possible on their way back from Killiecrankie, Robert Campbell of Glen Lyon cannot be called the instigator of this brutal act. He was not, as has sometimes been suggested, merely exacting his private revenge.

'The Massacre of Glencoe', when the chief of MacIain, a man of eighty years, and his wife were among the thirty-eight people who were killed, was the result of government orders.

CHAPTER V
Laird of Craigrostan

The Comer

Ben Lomond rises like a mighty giant protecting the loch at its feet. The land of the Comer[19] stretches from Gleann Dubh, on the east side of the mountain, over its north-west flank to Loch Lomond.

High above the loch lies the 'Shady Glen' of the well-known Highland song attributed to an imprisoned Jacobite who was about to be hanged. The high tops are beloved of red deer. The shy hind, as day breaks in the east, grazes downwind in a gentle breeze. In early June her calf will be born here and left safe in the heather, disguised by its spots, while its mother roams searching for food. In Rob Roy's time cattle were summered here. The ruins of shielings, where the women and children who herded them slept, can still be found alongside the burns. Now a pair of eagles soar undisturbed above land which, although a short way from Glasgow, as they fly, remains a wild and magic place.

Once over the watershed, the hill drops steeply to oak woods. Here live the wild goats which, from time immemorial, have grazed on the slopes of the Ben. Rob Roy must have been familiar with them. Perhaps he claimed the odd one for the pot! Today, walkers may catch a glimpse of them as they follow the West Highland Way along the shore.

In autumn, as the moor grass turns golden, stags roar defiance at others who try to encroach on their own parties of hinds. This is the time of migration as geese return from their nesting grounds further north. Skeins in v formation fly, honking noisily, following an old bird which recognises the landmarks of Highland lochs. Once over Ben Lomond many swoop down upon their wintering grounds around the mouth of the River Endrick at the south end of Loch Lomond.

The farmhouse of the Comer stands facing south-east down Gleann Dubh. The burn above the house, headwater of the massive River Forth, cascades down the side of Ben Lomond. In dry weather the water is clear as glass. The rocks of the stream bed near the house have been hollowed out to form the 'washtubs' of Rob Roy's time.

In the late 1600s, the people were self sufficient. They survived largely on salted beef and venison, some oatmeal and the milk from their cows. It was a hard life but they were mountain bred, used to rain and bitter wind. Gregor MacGregor, who farmed the Comer, had a daughter called Helen Mary. She married the third son of Donald MacGregor of Glengyle, known throughout the district for the colour of his hair as Rob Roy.

Marriage – 1693

The Register of Buchanan Parish proves that on the 1 January 1693 'Robert MacGregor and Marie MacGregor in this parish gave in their names to be proclaimed in order of marriage. Married at Coreklet.' [20]

At the time of his marriage, Rob Roy was twenty-two and his bride was about the same age. They were, in fact, distant cousins, and Helen Mary had been courted by Rob while she was living in her uncle Alasdair's house at Loch Arklet on the north side of Ben Lomond. No portrait of her exists and verbal accounts are vague. She is generally described as having black hair and a strong mind of her own. She certainly went like a tigress for Grahame of Killearn, the Duke of Montrose's factor, when, at a later date, he drove her from her home.

Her marriage to Rob Roy seems to have been a love match for, as the third son of a Jacobite chief, he had little to offer a young wife. Yet, within a few years, through a series of unforeseen circumstances, he found himself in possession of a Highland estate. Back in 1693, however, he and Helen Mary had been married for just six weeks when, on 9 February, the chain of events which was to alter their lives began. On that day, Rob Roy's first cousin, Gregor, chief of Clan Gregor, died aged only 32.

Inchcailloch

Islands were favoured places for burials in early times. Evil spirits could not cross water, or so it was believed, and from a practical sense neither could wolves nor other animals prone to digging up graves. Later, this applied to the body-snatchers who, by the eighteenth century, were actively plying their trade.

Inchcailloch, or *Inch-Cailleach* ('Island of the Old Woman'), the hereditary burial place of the chiefs of Clan Gregor, lies a short way off the east shore of Loch Lomond, almost opposite the village of Balmaha. It is just south of Craigrostan where Gregor had lived until he died. A quiet man, apparently with poor health, Gregor had an undistinguished life. Nonetheless, he was buried with all the honour due to a chief.

On the day of his funeral the sails of many birlinns converged on the island in the loch. Among them was that of Donald Glas, who had walked from Glengyle with his three sons to his boat at Inversnaid. Wrapped in their plaids, they sat huddled against the February wind on which the haunting strains of the pipes playing a lament floated across the winter dark water of the loch.

When all were gathered in the churchyard there was silence, save for waves lapping on the shore. Prayers were said in Gaelic by the minister before the Sennachie (or bard), in the same tongue, recited the pedigree of the man around whose resting place they stood. 'Gregor vic Callum vic Donnachie . . .' the names stretched on interminably back into the mists of time.

The funeral over, the mourners departed in their boats. The winter night fell and Inchcailloch lay silent save for the cry of a heron and the hoot of a hunting owl.

Craigrostan

Following the death of Gregor MacGregor the chiefship fell to his cousin, Archibald MacGregor of Kilmanan. Three months after his succession, in May 1693, Archibald negotiated with Sir Humphrey Colquhoun of Luss to purchase the lands of Craigrostan.[21]

He was planning the purchase for the younger of his two sons. However, hardly was the deal completed before the boy in question died. The older son wanted nothing to do with Craigrostan and his father, knowing the situation of Rob Roy and Helen Mary, to both of whom he was related, decided that Craigrostan should eventually be theirs.

The legal transaction was not completed when Rob began building his own house. Sited by the confluence of the Snaid burn with the Arklet Water, it was probably constructed by local people, most of whom belonged to the families of MacGregors who had lived on the east shore of Loch Lomond since the thirteenth century at least.

The estate of Craigrostan, comprising 6,720 acres, stretched from the Allt Rostan, near the head of Loch Lomond, almost to Rowardennan, a distance of some twelve miles. It included most of the west face of Ben Lomond, to the height of Loch Arklet which marked the eastern march. It was not good land. The small patches of corn, grown in the lower part of the glens above the loch, often produced little or nothing in a bad year. Potatoes had not yet become a common crop and so the people relied largely on milk, and the beef and venison which they salted down in tubs. It was a hard life, but the small tenant farmers, who were mostly MacGregors, could survive in most cases on the little they possessed.

On 14 May 1706, Sir Humphrey Colquhoun of Luss, as superior, eventually signed a charter granting the lands and barony with the office of 'baillerie' (magistrate) to Archibald Graham of Kilmanan, as the chief of Clan Gregor now was known. Three weeks later, on the 7th June, Kilmanan conveyed his newly acquired property rights to Robert Campbell, alias Rob Roy, who thus, as the holder of a barony, obtained the right to vote.[22]

Today, the east shore of Loch Lomond is traversed by the West Highland Way. Of the many people who walk along it perhaps not all are aware that this was the land of Rob Roy MacGregor, hero of the blockbuster film they will almost certainly have seen. Rob Roy's cave (one of the many in which he sometimes lived) overlooks the loch about a kilometre north of Inversnaid. From here, he had a bird's eye view of approaching enemy or friend.

The house which he built for his family stood in a little glen of its own, a short way above the landing place where his birlinn lay pulled up on the shore. Nothing remains of the house itself which was twice destroyed. Stones from it may have may have been used for the walls of nearby buildings such as the Inversnaid Hotel.

In Rob Roy's time there were little groups of cottages, some built of rough stones, others of turf, in Craigrostan. According to the *Graham of Gartmore Manuscript* there were one hundred and fifty families living there in the late sixteenth century, the majority of them were MacGregors. The smoke from the chimneys on a still day must have hung low above the loch. The surrounding hillside was then covered with deciduous trees, mostly birch, oak, rowan and mountain ash. Now it is largely forested with dark swathes of sitka spruce. Above the proud peak of Ben Lomond remains the familiar landmark, which to Rob Roy meant home.

The Atholl Raids

Rob Roy and Helen Mary had been married a bare six months when, on 15 June 1693, the Scottish Parliament renewed the Act of Proscription against Clan Gregor. The reasons for this are obscure. The chiefs, both of Clan Gregor and the cadet branches, had sworn the oath of allegiance to King William, and Donald Glas, who had raised a regiment for King James, had been released and pardoned eighteen months before.

Rob Roy is known to have rented an extensive stretch of grazing in Balquhidder at about this time. As a tacksman,[23] he had to acknowledge the authority of the Marquis of Atholl, who held the superiority of that district. This placed him in a difficult position with the Earl of Breadalbane, reputedly so furious over Atholl's acquisition of Glen Lyon that he set upon Lord Murray (Atholl's eldest son) with his fists when they met in Holyrood House.

Rob Roy, however, had been high in Breadalbane's favour since retrieving his cows. Keen to maintain his protection, he had taken his name of Campbell when that of MacGregor was again proscribed. Breadalbane for his part encouraged him to raid the Atholl lands. Lord Murray did not pay 'mail' for the protection of the Glengyle Watch and therefore Rob Roy, even if technically his vassal, had not bound himself to any form of obligation to protect his stock in Atholl.

Thus, in the autumn of 1694, when the sheep were fat with grass, a flock of no less than three hundred and fifty vanished overnight from Glen Almond, part of the Atholl estates.

The little town of Crieff was alive with rumour on the next market day. Lord Murray, fuming about what had occurred, described his loss to John Menzies of Struan, one of the Atholl tenants in Glen Quaich, whom he happened to meet by the Cross. Menzies made matters worse by telling him that he had only himself to blame.

'Our friend sheep Robbie would likely ken o' your wethers [male sheep] – if indeed he had not his own hand in them,' he sneered in a sarcastic way.

Such a good story, told by those returning from the market, soon reached Rob Roy's ears.

'"Sheep Robbie"!' he snorted in fury. 'Royal's my race – it will be "cattle Robbie" when next he speaks of me,' whereupon that night the whole of Menzie's herd of cattle in Glen Quaich disappeared without trace.

These are just two of the many legends associated with Rob Roy's name but an entry in the *Atholl Papers*, dated 25 May 1695, proves Lord Murray's antagonism towards him. He writes that word has reached him 'about one Rob Campbel, a son of that Lieut. Col. MacGregor who cheated my father, and he and his family have continued to do all they could against me . . . I have sent a party to apprehend that Rob Campbel. I have not yett heard [what] they have done. I believe Bread: indeed is his friend because he has taken that name, and his [lordship] has espoused his interest when he was pursued before the justiciary court, wherefor I wish none of his lps frends at Dunkeld may gett notice I imployed about him.'[24]

The party sent out to capture Rob Roy was commanded by a man called Duncan MacEown. Rob Roy is said to have been taken prisoner in Balquhidder, in his own house, a clear indication that he was living there at that time. MacEown must have been careless, or else amazingly naive for, having ordered his men to heave their captive on to the back of a horse, he did not tell them to tie his hands. What happened thereafter was predictable . . .

Loch Lubnaig

Loch Lubnaig, the loch of the bays, winds its way from below Strathyre for a distance of about six miles before it narrows into the Pass of Leny through which the water surges down to the River Teith. Today, the lower slopes of the mountains above the loch are dark with sitka spruce. Above them, the hillside juts towards the sky, so precipitous that on a still day the water below is edged with the shadow of trees and towering rocks. To the south east the great peak of Ben Ledi, beloved of the ancient sun worshippers, catches the first light of dawn.

The main road now follows the contour of the loch, but in the late seventeenth century only a rough track ran on the drier and higher ground, where the burns were easier to cross. Rob Roy, familiar with every inch, knew that there was one place, so narrow and dangerous on a near perpendicular slope, that horses could only move in single file. Swaying about in the saddle, pretending he could barely ride, he waited until the spot was reached. Then, leaping upwards from the stirrups, he seized a branch hanging over the track and was up the bank and away. The soldiers, confused by frightened horses, took a long time to dismount and by the time they had scrambled up the hill Rob Roy was out of sight.

The First Submission

The *Chronicle of the Atholl and Tullibardine Families* proves that Rob Roy made his peace with Lord Murray within a matter of weeks. Astute man of business that he was, he realised the advantages of submitting to someone of great influence who was also the superior of his land. Thus, on 22 June 1695, he subscribed to a bond of which the following is an extract.

Be it known to all men, Be thir presents me Robert Roy Campbell, sometime McGrigor, sone to Lieut Col McGrigor, ffor as much as ane noble Lord, John Lord Murray, is pleased to receive me into his Lops favour, notwithstanding of my many ungrateful deportments and undecent carriages for some yeares by past. Therefor I the said Robert Roy Campbell as principal and Alexr McDonnell, Laird of Glengarrie and Alex, McDonald, brother german to John McDonald of Glencoe, as cautioners for me . . . That the sd Robert Campbell shall hereafter, and in all time coming, not only behave himselfe as a loyall and dutifull subject under this present government but also as ane honest, faithful and obedient servant to the Noble lord . . . and shall live honestly, peaceably and quietly in all time coming, and that under the penalty of ane thousand pounds scotts money, to be payed to his Lop by us in case of failzie . . . [25]

This document was signed in front of six witnesses, who included the future Lord Lovat, subscribing himself in this instance as simply 'Sim. Fraser'.

Imprisonment

Despite having reconciled himself to Lord Murray, Rob Roy was arrested and thrown into the Tolbooth in Glasgow later in the year. The crime for which he was seized is unrecorded, but he narrowly escaped deportation. On 19 December 1695, the Privy Council ordered 'Robert McGregor prisoner in Glasgow to be sent along with some others to Flanders.'

Somehow, perhaps by bribery, he managed to escape.[26]

Farmer, Drover and Keeper of the Watch

The last years of the seventeenth century were hard for anyone in Scotland whose living depended on the land. The years from 1696 to 1699 were renowned for some of the worst weather and consecutive bad harvests that had ever been known. Many families suffered, both from the effects of the climate and the recent civil war.

Donald Glas of Glengyle, already a widower, lost his two eldest sons. Duncan, the second one, appears to have died shortly after his release from Edinburgh prison in 1690. His elder brother, Iain, who had stayed at home during the Rising, nonetheless died in 1700, leaving a boy of thirteen as his heir. Donald Glas himself, still suffering from the hardships of imprisonment, died two years later in 1702.

Rob Roy, as Donald's only surviving son, then became guardian or tutor of his brother Iain's son, Gregor, known as 'Gregor Ghlun Dubh' because he had been born with a large black spot on his knee.

In 1701, Archibald MacGregor of Kilmanan, chief of Clan Gregor and calling himself 'Graham', had resigned the lands of Craigrostan to Rob Roy. Further to this, in 1704, he gave him the lands of Inversnaid.

Thus, the red-headed Robert, who had been born a near penniless youngest son, was now a man of substance. With more than 6,000 acres on the east shore of Loch Lomond, albeit much of it poor land, he also continued to rent the grazing in Balqhidder on which he maintained large herds of cows.

However, the business of cattle-dealing kept him away from home, as did the Glengyle Watch for which his wife, Helen Mary, had sometimes to collect the 'mail' during his absence. His terms of business are not known but it is recorded that in 1741 his nephew, Gregor Ghlun Dubh,

> agreed with various landholders of estates in the counties of Perth, Stirling, and Dumbarton, to recover cattle stolen from them, or to pay the value within six months of the loss being intimated . . . in consideration of a payment of £5 on each £100 of valued rent, which was not a very heavy insurance. Petty thefts were not included in the contract; but the theft of one horse, or one head of black cattle, or of sheep exceeding the number of six, fell under the agreement.[27]

The same account tells us that 'Rob Roy's profits upon such contracts brought him in a considerable revenue in money or cattle, of which he made popular use; for he was publicly liberal as well as privately beneficent.'

Obviously, he was prospering, for in March 1703 he bought much of Glengyle from the Marquis of Montrose for his ward and nephew Gregor. The boy being yet a minor, Rob Roy purchased the land in his own name.

Travelling throughout the country and picking up news at the markets, Rob Roy acquired a unique knowledge of what was taking place. Letters in the *Atholl Papers* prove that he was acting as an intelligence agent to the Marquis of Atholl (made a duke by Queen Anne in 1703) at this time.

Simon Fraser, witness of Rob Roy's submission to Atholl, had convinced the Duke of Argyll and the Duke of Queensberry, the Secretary of State for Scotland, that Atholl was involved in a plot against Queen Anne. Supposedly, he was supporting a French invasion on behalf of the 'Old Pretender', son of James VII & II, and had written secretly to Louis XIV of France.

Rob Roy is said to have been offered a bribe to bear false witness, instead he sent a warning to the Duke of Atholl through his wife.

On February 2nd 1704, the Duchess wrote to her husband from Holyrood House that she had seen Rob Roy who had given her some information about the plot, and that he was convinced he could tell enough if he liked. [28]

No one was more adept at pressing home an advantage than Rob Roy. He was also expert at playing off the rivalry between the great landlords of his day. The War of the Spanish Succession had just begun and his father's old friend, Colonel Alexander Campbell of Fonab, at the instigation of the young Duke of Argyll, was looking for recruits for his Independent Company. That his methods of doing so were sometimes circumspect was intimated to the Duke of Atholl by Rob Roy.

The letter, headed 'Glengyle, ye 20 May 1704', informed him that: 'In Your Grace's absence Fownab prest [forced into military service] tuo of your men and sent them to Edinburgh for recreits; yr names be John and Duncane McEune Voire, late McGrigors in Glen Lyon.'

Then, significantly, he adds, 'Duncane, living at ye time under ye Earle Badalbin [Breadalbane] was brought back. John remains still there. Your Grace was pleased to protect these two men formerly. Therefor I humbly beg that yr Grace may be pleased to liberat this poor man, who hath left a wyfe and maney smal children behind him. If not, Fownab May heirafter dispose of Yr Grace's men as if they were his oune.'[29]

Atholl's reply, if he made one, has been lost. Nonetheless, it seems safe to presume that the mere insinuation of Breadalbane's authority outmatching his own would have been enough to ensure that John McEune was promptly returned to Glen Lyon.

The deal with the Marquis of Montrose over the sale of Glengyle provides the first intimation of Rob Roy's dealings with the man with whom he later became so deeply involved. James Graham, Marquis of Montrose, a very good-looking, exceedingly ambitious young man, had just bought the vast property of the Lennox from the Duke of Lennox (the illegitimate son of Charles II). His new lands stretched across the central valley of Scotland from Loch Lomond to the Campsie Fells and so it is probable that he sold Glengyle to partly finance the deal.

Montrose, keen to make money in any way possible, was also involved in the cattle trade. He employed Rob Roy, by now known as one of the most astute dealers in Scotland, to buy cattle wherever he could find them and to sell them at the big autumn fairs.

It was a fluctuating trade, thanks to the political unrest in Scotland which followed Queen Anne's succession in 1702. The Act of Settlement, passed by the English Government without Scottish assent, declared that on the Queen's death the crown would go to Sophia Dorothea, Electress of Hanover, the granddaughter of James VI.

In retaliation, the Scottish Parliament passed the Act of Security in 1704 enacting that the crowns of England and Scotland should not go to the same person unless he or she be descended from the Royal House of Stewart and a Protestant. Animosity increased until it seemed that the two countries were on the verge of civil war.

The English Government had already caused outrage in Scotland by prohibiting trade with the American countries and now, in what seems like incredible folly, it passed what was called an Alien Act which declared that the sale of all Scottish cattle and sheep to England was prohibited unless the Scottish Parliament accepted the Act of Settlement by Christmas Day, 1705.

Montrose, holding high office in the Scottish Parliament, became Lord President of the Privy Council in 1705. Sales of cattle had plummeted in Scotland to the point where several of the dealers were forced out of business but, thanks to his inside knowledge that the Alien Act was about to be repealed, he and Rob Roy achieved a spectacular coup. Rob Roy bought cattle at Crieff for no more than 6s and 8d each and sold them again in England for £4. The implication of insider dealing, although obviously made, did not in those days result in political disgrace.

CHAPTER VI

The Treaty of Union, 1707

A Country on the Verge of War

The Treaty of Union was signed on the 16 January 1707. Rob Roy, both Jacobite and fervent patriot, detested his country's loss of independence. Nonetheless, he saw the advantage of free trade with England as far as cattle dealing was concerned. For this reason, he followed the lead of that most devious of men, Lord Breadalbane, in refusing to commit himself to plans for a Rising in favour of James Edward, son of James VII and II. The situation changed, however, when in the spring of 1707 a secret agent from the court of St Germains appeared in Scotland to negotiate with leaders of the Jacobite cause.

The Gathering at Kinloch Rannoch

In April 1707, Colonel Hooke, an old officer of Dundee's, arrived. He came pretending to be a cattle dealer when his real object was to promote a Rising to restore the Stewart king to the throne. Word went out of a hunting match at Kinloch Rannoch to which all chiefs of known Jacobite affinity were bidden to attend. Breadalbane is said to have been among them. Likewise Rob Roy.

Reputedly, two documents were discussed and signed. The first was a Memorial to the King of France, assuring him of much support in Scotland for opposition to the Treaty of Union and asking for his aid in terms of both money, arms and men. This was conveyed to France

Loch Lomond and Craigrostan in winter

Loch Lubnaig, Perthshire

Snow and ice on Perthshire hills

Highland cattle at Aultbea

by Hooke, who assured the assembled company that a fleet to convey a large body of French soldiers to Scotland would be ready to sail in four months' time. The second was a Bond of Association signed by those who committed themselves to upholding the exiled king's cause.

The names attached to this pledge are said to have included 'some of the noblest of the Highland chiefs'. Among them were those of John Campbell, Earl of Breadalbane, and Robert Campbell, better known as Rob Roy.

Attempted Invasion of Scotland by James VIII and III

In March 1708 James Edward Stewart was aboard one of the fleet of ships which set sail from France with the capture of Edinburgh as their aim. The French crews, confused in darkness, however, missed the entrance to the Firth of Forth. Discovering their mistake, they put about only to find themselves faced by the ships of the English Navy commanded by Admiral Byng. The wind being against them, they sailed back into the North Sea where a storm struck and many ships were sunk. The invasion which never took place thus came to an inglorious end.

A few Jacobites were tried for high treason. Among them was Rob Roy's erstwhile adversary, Archibald Stirling of Garden, who, together with some other Stirlingshire lairds, had ridden towards Edinburgh to support the expected landing of James VIII and III. All were acquitted for lack of evidence of any criminal intent.

The Bond of Association, signed at Kinloch Rannoch, with its damning evidence of treachery against Queen Anne was, however, still with Breadalbane. And that nobleman, most consummate of all double-dealers, was now rumoured to have 'turned his coat'.

Dal Righ

Through one of his many connections, word reached Rob Roy that his cousin, John Campbell of Glen Lyon (son of Robert Campbell his mother's brother), on the orders of Breadalbane, was to deliver the Bond of Association to the Commanding Officer at Fort William. From there, it was taken by an armed party of soldiers to Edinburgh for perusal by the Scottish Secretary of State.

Rob Roy allegedly spent an evening drinking with his cousin and found out what he had done. He then began to work out the best way and the best place for the document to be retrieved.

The field of *Dal Righ*, just south of Tyndrum, translated from the Gaelic means 'field of the king'. It takes its name from the battle that was fought here in 1306 between King Robert the Bruce and the MacDougalls of Lorn. Swords and pikes, collected after the fight, are said to have been thrown into the little loch beside the field which then became known as 'Loch an Arm'. It was on the narrow path beside the loch that Bruce had killed three assailants who had leapt upon him from the bank above. It was a natural place for an ambush, as Rob Roy was well aware.

The mounted company of soldiers, riding south from Fort William on their way to Edinburgh, were forced to proceed in single file along the shore of the loch. Suddenly, from the deep heather above, men armed with claymores surrounded them, blocking any means of escape. The young officer in command ordered them to stand aside but one of their number, a swarthy man with red hair, evidently their leader, ordered him to hand over his despatches if he valued his life.

The unfortunate ensign had little or no option and did as he was told. Rob Roy opened the bundle, removed the Bond of Association, gave him back the rest of the papers, and waved him on his way. The young officer put spurs to his horse and rode hard to Edinburgh where he was cashiered. Hardly had he vanished before Rob Roy was tearing the Bond in small pieces and throwing them to the wind.

Strathfillan

Strathfillan, the wide glen running south-east from Tyndrum to Crianlarich, takes its name from St Fillan, a Celtic saint who was the nephew of St Conan and connected with St Adamnan, biographer and near contemporary of St Columba.

King Robert the Bruce believed that it was St Fillan's mummified arm, taken to the battlefield, which brought him his great victory at Bannockburn. In gratitude, he founded an Augustinian Priory on the site of St Fillan's Celtic chapel in 1314. The pool in the river below the now ruined priory is said to have been blessed by the saint. It was believed to contain healing water and pilgrims came there from afar. In Rob Roy's time, according to legend, it became a ducking pond for a man who had wrongfully taken the land of a poor laird in the glen. The villain of the piece is said to have been a Campbell.

The story runs that Rob Roy sent his men to waylay him in Glenorchy 'at a defile which wound along the craggy cliffs of Ben Cruachan'. Making him prisoner, they took him to Tyndrum where Rob Roy made him sign a letter restoring the lands to their rightful owner. Having done this, he led the thief to St Fillan's pool 'and ducking him heartily, told him, that from the established virtues of that pool, a dip in it might improve his honour, so that he would not again rob a poor man of his lands.'[30]

The Beggar at the Ford of Dalree

Some years later a party of soldiers arrived in Tyndrum searching for Rob Roy. A beggar, who claimed that he had been cheated by him, offered to lead them to his hiding place for the price of five pounds. This ragged individual, hump-backed and wrapped in his plaid, led them down Strathfillan to the ford of Dalree. Despite his frail appearance, the soldiers forced him to carry them across the river for the sum of a penny each. He did not seem to feel the weight of them, however, muskets and all, for he took the smaller men two at a time, charging a half-penny for each.

Reaching Crianlarich, he silently indicated a thatched house where, in a hoarse whisper, he told them they would find Rob Roy and his men asleep. It would be easy to capture them as their arms were in the building next door.

Taking him at his word, the officer deployed his men round the house as he, his sergeant and two men, were guided by the beggar under a low threshold and into a small room. The officer looked round bewildered, eyes stinging from the smoke of a peat fire, while the beggar, the promised five pounds now in his sporran, seized his hand in gratitude and held it in a vice-like grip. Suddenly, it seemed from nowhere, the room was full of Highland men, armed with swords and daggers pointing at his throat. Before they knew what had happened, he and the soldiers with him were seized and bound with ropes. The beggar, going to the door, then called in the others, two at a time, who suffered the same fate. After they were all secured, the beggar – who, of course, was none other than Rob Roy – gave them a good meal of porridge, confiscated their weapons and sent them off. No doubt, they cursed their deception and dreaded their return to barracks, but at least they trudged down the boggy track through Strathfillan both well fed and dry shod. Later, recounting the story, those with a sense of humour may even have enjoyed a good laugh.

The Master Drover

Montrose, created a duke by Queen Anne in April 1707, was now Rob Roy's biggest employer. Other Lowland landowners, witnessing his success, followed suit and Rob Roy became the biggest cattle dealer in the Highlands of Scotland and the Isles. Although he travelled extensively, he could not control so large a business on his own. He increasingly employed drovers who travelled the length of Scotland and ferried cattle across to the mainland from many of the Western Isles.

The honesty of these men was legendary. The drovers collected cattle, often even single beasts from the cottars. Once the animals were sold they returned with the money in their sporrans and the owners received to the nearest farthing whatever they were owed. However, wealth, or the promise of it, corrupts, and Rob Roy, for all his shrewdness, in one case picked the wrong man.

In 1708, Donald, the second of Rob's late brother Iain's two sons (younger brother of Gregor Ghlun Dubh), reached the age of seventeen. Rob Roy, who had reared both boys as his own, now took the tack or lease of the farm of Monachyle Tuarach. This wooded, north-facing hill in Balquhidder on the south shore of Loch Doine was owned by the Duke of Atholl. Donald was inexperienced and Rob thus installed one of his chief drovers, a man called Alastair MacDonald, as farm manager. He believed him to be honest, having known him for several years.

The Treaty of Union, unpopular as it was in Scotland, at least opened up the English markets to Scottish trade. The demand for the small Scottish cattle, which did particularly well when fattened up on better pasture, was increasing and Rob Roy decided to expand his already profitable business still more. Papers in the possession of the Society of Antiquaries include a contract with the Duke of Montrose, dated December, 1711, and signed 'Ro. Campbell'. By this he pledged himself to deliver 'sixtie good and sufficient Kintail Highland cowes, betwixt the age of five and nine years, at fourtene pounds Scotts per peice, with ane bull to the bargane, and that at the head dykes of Buchanan upon the twenty-eight day of May nixt to come under the pain of tuo hundereth merks Scotts money in caise of fealzie attour performance.'[31]

The money needed to buy sixty head of cattle at fourteen pounds a beast amounted to £840. They must have sold well because next year an even bigger deal was struck between the successful business partners Rob Roy and Montrose. Capital on an even larger scale was necessary and so, in the summer of 1712, Rob Roy 'wadsetted' (mortgaged) his own property of Craigrostan to the Duke. Other landlords, keen to take advantage of the profits being made, also advanced him money to the point where he received the then enormous sum of about £1,000.

The loans were obtained before the cattle (driven to the *airidhs* in May) were brought down fat with grass, ready to be taken to the autumn sales. Rob Roy, entrusting most of it to MacDonald, now his chief drover, sent him off to buy the herds. It was the last he ever saw of him. Both he and the money disappeared.

What actually happened remains a mystery to this day. MacDonald is said to have bought the cattle on bills of exchange (the equivalent of cheques) and then sold them himself. It is possible that he emigrated, either to Europe or America, as many were doing at that time. Had he remained in this country, Rob Roy, through the grapevine of the dealers, would certainly have tracked him down.

Meanwhile in Scotland, rumour ran wild. Rob Roy was said to have disappeared with the money to the Western Isles. Other stories maintained that he was on his way to Rome to the court of the exiled James VIII and III to persuade him to attempt another invasion of Scotland financed by the stolen money. The first assumption was partly correct. Rob Roy was in the Outer Hebrides searching in vain for MacDonald and for two other men who owed him money.

He returned to the mainland to discover that the Edinburgh *Evening Courant*, on four consecutive days, namely 18–21 June 1712, had printed an order for his arrest. 'All Magistrates and Officers of her Majesty's forces are entreated to seize upon the said Rob Roy.' His creditors had foreclosed upon him. He was a wanted man.

His father's old friend, Colonel Alexander Campbell of Fonab, in command of Argyll's Independent Company, was ordered to take him prisoner. In desperation, Rob Roy wrote to the Duke of Atholl. The letter, headed 'Port'nellan, 27 January 1713', runs:

> I am hopeful Your Grace Has heard how ye Duke of Montrose is offering to ruine me upon the accompt of cautionrie yt I engaged to his Grace. I have offered him the whole principle soume with a yeir's rent, which he positively refuses ye same . . . his Grace thought it fitt to procure ane order from the Queen's advocate to Funab, to secure me . . . Funab is still promesing to put this order in executione; but if I can his Grace and he will not doe it. God knowes but there is vast differs between Dukes . . . Blessed be God that it is not ye Athole men that is after me, altho' it were if your Grace would send me the least foot boy I would come without any protection. Your Grace was always charitable and kynd to me beyond my deservings. If your Grace woulde speake to ye advocate to countermand his order, since its contrary to the Law, it would ease me very much of my troubles, and I beg pardone for this trouble and for the superscriptione hereof, and I am,
>   Your Grace's servant while I am alive, Rob Roy. [32]

Alas, this appeal came to nothing. Rob Roy's friends in high places seem to have been the first to desert him in the desperate situation in which he now was placed.

A month later, on 28 February 1713, the first of five adjudications of his goods and lands were given against Rob Roy in favour of Sir John Shaw of Greenock, the Duke of Montrose, Graham of Gorthie, James Graham (writer in Glasgow), Campbell of Blythswood, MacFarlane, Buchanan and Montgomery.[33] In addition to this he was declared an outlaw and publicly put to the horn.[34]

Montrose did not wait to seize the estate of Craigrostan which Rob Roy had mortgaged to him only in the previous June. At the beginning of March he sent instructions to his factor, John Grahame of Killearn, to take possession of all Rob Roy's property at Craigrostan – his house and its contents, his animals and, most importantly, all the grain stocked within the barns. Grahame, acting in his capacity of Sheriff Substitute for Dumbartonshire, led a party of soldiers to carry out the eviction as he was told. Helen Mary is said to have physically attacked him as she was driven from her home at Inversnaid. Stories that she was raped by the soldiers are unproven, but she certainly cursed them in Gaelic and may well have set about Grahame before they pulled her away.

The house which Rob Roy had built for her was left partly destroyed to prevent her trying to return to it once Grahame and his men were gone. They took everything they could carry and every beast that could move they drove away. Helen Mary and her three sons, of whom the youngest was only seven, were left without a roof over their heads and with nothing to keep them alive. Fortunately, both she and her boys were strong and used to tramping the hills. It was not far to Loch Katrine where she took refuge either with one of her uncles or with their young chief, Gregor Ghlun Dubh, in Glengyle.

Rob Roy is believed to have been in England, trying to collect money from his creditors, when this outrage to his family occurred. Returning to find himself ruined, he swore to wreak vengeance on the man he held mostly responsible, Montrose.

CHAPTER VII

The Rising of 1715

The Outlaw, Rob Roy

Rob Roy was a man of forty when he was made an outlaw. He was left without possessions, home or money and was not allowed to trade.

Lord Breadalbane, devious as he was, at this time of crisis now proved to be a friend. Breadalbane, who as ever had an eye to his own interests, saw Rob Roy as a useful ally in curbing the ambitions of Montrose. Taking him under his protection, he gave him a house called Corrycharmeg, on the south side of Glen Dochart, where Rob Roy lived for a short while.

As for his family, it may have been at this time that his children went to school at Acharn on the south shore of Loch Tay where they apparently boarded with relations. James, the eldest, had been born in 1695 and would now be eighteen; a man of the world. Coll was three years younger and Duncan was nine. The youngest son, Robin Oig, was not born until 1716.

Later, Breadalbane gave Rob Roy Auchinchisallan, which has since been proved by Dr MacGregor Hutcheson to have actually been the present farm of Auch. This lies about 5 miles north of Tyndrum to the east of and below the A82. A track from Auch leads up to the head of Glen Lyon. The MacDonalds of Glencoe came home down this way after raiding Glen Lyon, following the battle of Killiecrankie in 1689. It must also have been a familiar road to Rob Roy.

Queen Anne died on 1 August 1714. Prince George, Elector of Brunswick-Luneburg (son of Sophia Dorothea, granddaughter of James VI & I) was then immediately proclaimed king. In France, Prince James Edward, son of James VII & II, asked Louis XIV to supply him with men and money to invade Scotland, but the French king, now old and feeble, refused. He died on 1 September, almost as the Elector of Brunswick arrived in England as George I.

One of the Scottish nobles who journeyed to London to the court of the new king was John, Earl of Mar. Largely ignored, he was much affronted, and returned to Scotland to head the Jacobite cause. In August, he issued a summons to all the clan chiefs to assemble at another so-called hunting party at Braemar. There, plans were made for a Rising which would place Prince James Edward on the throne instead of the German king. The Duke of Atholl declared for King George, but the Marquis of Tullibardine (his eldest surviving son), and his brother Lord George Murray, pretending they were going to visit their grandmother, the Duchess of Hamilton, instead rode north for Braemar.

On 6 September Mar raised the Standard of Prince James Edward at the Castleton of Braemar. Three days later, on the 9th, he issued a Declaration and a call to arms, followed by a manifesto declaring his intentions to bring the son of James VII & II to Scotland, and there to proclaim him king.

Rob Roy as Intelligence Officer

Rob Roy's reputation for efficiency and promptness had become a by-word throughout the Highlands and the Isles. Now, at the age of forty-four, he possessed a near unique knowledge of the country and had built up an intelligence network to the point where little occurred of importance of which he was unaware. Most people, great lords included, knew that if they needed something done quickly, with no questions asked, the now grey-haired MacGregor was their man.

The Earl of Mar, aware of this, made him a special agent throughout the length of his campaign. From Braemar, he sent him to raise recruits on Deeside and Speyside where MacGregors had been living for almost a hundred years. Following the proscription of Clan Gregor in 1604, Rob Roy's own grandfather had led about three hundred members of the clan to Morayshire, where they had settled. Also, at much the same time, MacGregors of Roro in Glen Lyon had been given shelter and employed as foresters by the Duke of Gordon in Strathavon. In all, they amounted to a considerable number of men and Mar sent Rob Roy on a recruiting mission, which appears to have been successful.

At the end of August, Rob Roy was in Aberdeen where he stayed with his cousin Dr James Gregory, a professor of medicine at King's College. The family had adopted this name when that of MacGregor had been proscribed, and James was the first of three generations to win fame in the medical world. His son, James, later known as Gregory Secondus, was at that time a boy of eight years old. Rob Roy, with the best intentions, pleaded with his father to let him take him away 'to make a man of him' but his father, saying he was delicate, managed to put an end to such a ploy.

Attack on Inveraray

On 28 September, Mar occupied Perth and established his headquarters in the town. Meanwhile, in Stirling, no more than 30 miles away, the Duke of Argyll, commander-in-chief of the Hanoverian army in Scotland, waited in readiness to confront him when the chance occurred.

Hoping that Argyll would be drawn from Stirling to defend his own land, Mar ordered General Gordon to attack Inveraray. With a force of MacDonalds, MacLeans and Camerons and some MacGregors, Gordon marched upon the little town which then stood in and about the garden of the present Inveraray Castle. The old castle, a square hall-house, dating from the late fifteenth century, was close to the castle entrance of today. In 1715, it was held by Argyll's brother, Archibald Earl of Ilay (later the 3rd duke) with Colonel Campbell of Fonab as his second in command.

Gordon encamped his force at the foot of Glen Shira on the lovely stretch of meadow by the river. It is known locally as the 'Boshang' because Mary Queen of Scots, when staying with her half-sister the Countess of Argyll, exclaimed, 'Quelle beau champ!' as she rode into the glen.

From the camp, the men of Gordon's army looked down Loch Fyne. The company of MacGregors, commanded by Gregor Ghlun Dubh of Glengyle, included among its officers none other than his uncle Rob Roy. The story goes that the sight of a heavily laden ship, beating up the loch against the wind, was a temptation too hard to resist. Rob Roy is said to have led a party of his men round the head of the loch to a point where she came close to the shore. Wading out, with muskets held high above their heads to keep the powder dry, they boarded her and made her crew prisoners in the name of King James.

Their triumph was short lived, however, for Gordon, without siege weapons, could not subdue the castle. A skirmish which resulted from a Highland soldier giving a password in Gaelic to a Lowland man in the defending force, fooled him into thinking that the town was being relieved and he gave orders to withdraw.

The MacGregors, under orders, abandoned their prize ship. They did so with great reluctance, yet rumours were soon circulating among his enemies that Rob Roy had only released it because of an agreement with Argyll.

The siege over, Gordon returned to Perthshire. His mission had proved a failure as the Duke 'Red John of the Battles' had refused to be drawn from Stirling, leaving the defence of Inveraray to his brother and Colonel Campbell of Fonab. Ensconced at his headquarters, he waited to confront the Jacobite army commanded by the Earl of Mar.

MacGregor Raids on Loch Lomond

An account of the Rebellion was written in 1745 by a clergyman, the Reverend Mr Peter Rae, who must have been a young man at the time. He describes how, at the beginning of October, the Captain of Clanranald joined MacDonell of Glengarry:

> who sometime before was reinforced with 300 of the Mcgregours and Glenco-Men . . . This clan of the McGregours had about the End of September, broke out in Rebellion under the Command of Gregor McGregiour [sic] of Glengyle, nephew to that notorious robber Rob

Roy, and in a considerable body made an excursion on their neighbours, especially on Buchannan and the Heads of Monteith, and coming on them unawares disarmed them. Upon Michaelmas day they made themselves Masters of the Boats on the Water of Endrick and Loch Lomond, and about seventy men of them possessed themselves of Inchmurrin, a large Isle in the said Loch whence about midnight they came ashore on the paroch of Bonhill three miles above Dumbarton but being alarmed by the ringing of bells in several paroches and the discharge of two great Guns from the Castle of Dumbarton to warn the country, they made haste to the boats and returned to the Isle where they did considerable damage.[35]

The minister then describes how the MacGregors pulled all the boats on the lochside up the hill where they hid them among low-growing bushes above Inversnaid. They then returned briefly to Mar's camp before mustering at Craigrostan on 10 October.

The local lairds decided to take action against them. Three long-boats and four pinnaces were brought from the Men of War then lying in the Clyde and with them came four pateraroes,[36] two gunners and a hundred seamen 'stout and well armed'. Other boats were collected and the entire little fleet was towed up the River Leven by horses to Loch Lomond where a party of soldiers, including the Paisley Volunteers, went on board.

In the meantime, the men of Dumbarton were marching up the north-west side of the Loch, while behind came a party of armed local landowners, headed by the Honourable John Campbell of Mamore, uncle of the Duke of Argyll. Arriving at Luss, they were joined by Sir Humphrey Colquhoun and 'forty or fifty stately fellows in their short hose and belted plaids, armed each of them with a well fix'd gun on his shoulder, a strong handsome target, with a sharp pointed steel of about half an ell in length screwed into the navel of it, on his left arm; a sturdy claymore by his side, and a pistol or two with a dirk and knife on his belt'.

The minister does not say so but they must have embarked in the boats for continuing the next day [Thursday, 13 October] at about noon they came to 'Innersnaat, the Place of Danger, where the Paisley men [and others] with the greatest intrepidity leap'd on shore, got up to the Top of the Mountains and stood a considerable time beating their drums . . . but no enemy appearing, they went on in quest of their boats,' which they eventually found and 'hurled down to the Loch'. The boats were towed back to Dumbarton and anchored under the protection of the cannons of the castle.[37]

According to the minister, 'the pinnaces discharging their pateraroes, and the men their small arms, made such a thundering noise . . . that the Mcgregiours were cowed and frighted away to the rest of the Rebels, who were encamped at Streathphillen [*sic*]' where, about the 18th October, 'they were joined by Stuart of Appin with 250 men, Sir John McLean with 400, McDougal of Lorn with about 50, and a part of Breadalbane's men [2,400 in all]'.

General Gordon, after his failed attempt on Inveraray, was at Drummond Castle in Strathearn by the beginning of November. He joined Mar at Auchterarder on the 11th and was ordered, with his 3,000 men of the Highland clans to advance and take Dunblane. Argyll, however, beat him to it, his advance guard seizing the town.

Argyll's army had been reinforced with men from Ireland but his strength was still not enough to hold the line of the Forth. Therefore, he decided to attack before the enemy could reach the river. He arrayed his army on sloping ground above the house of Kippenross, while Mar deployed his force at the Bridge of Kinbuck.

Between them lay a stretch of moorland. They were less than three miles apart.

Sheriffmuir

The battle of Sheriffmuir was fought on 13 November 1715. The result was indecisive. The right wing of each side defeated the other's left. The incident which is now most clearly remembered is that Rob Roy refused to fight. 'It is said that he stood on a hill in the centre of the Highland position when the right wing had cut to pieces Argyll's left wing, while the clans on the left of Mar's army were completely routed, yet Rob Roy could not be prevailed upon to charge.'[38]

Jacobites have since claimed that he had been bribed to stay out of the battle by the Duke of Argyll. One source insists that Argyll paid him eighty guineas not to join the Earl of Mar.[39] More factually, it seems that for some reason he came late upon the field and in the confusion, believing the battle lost, decided it was folly to throw away more lives.

It is, however, on record that he raided the baggage trains of both armies. Reputedly, when asked afterwards for whom he had fought he said, 'Neither King Geordie or King Jamie. Only King Spulzie.'[40]

This may have been an invention of his enemies. Yet his inaction certainly meant that some poor MacGregor families fared better that winter than they might otherwise have done.

CHAPTER VIII

Continued Rebellion, 1715–16

On 21 November 1715, Rob Roy wrote to the Duke of Argyll in the following terms:

May it please your Grace. The Bearer of this will give you sufficient intelligence upon the late movements of the people here and as I cannot put down on paper I hope you will forgive me at this juncture but must take the risque of the messenger coming at you – I hope that nothing will come out, that will make so much turmoil as I do not think the army of Mar can come to so much against your Grace's men if they only all come out. As to what your Grace may know about the people here from other people be very careful as MN and GD were sent Yesterday to make false news to the people in the district from which I know that they have sufficient designs to make grievous injury to the forces under you if they can. They were both sent with Proclamations to be issued and as I send this by a quicker route you shd give orders to detayn them at the Bridge or wherever found.

    I shall have mair for you when I get the matter on hand settled with them —— [41]

This is the first indication of Rob Roy's association with the Duke of Argyll. The letter is important for what it indicates rather than what it actually says. 'The bearer of this will give you sufficient intelligence . . . I cannot put down on paper.' What news did the bearer bring which was so highly secret that it was dangerous to convey it in writing in case the messenger might be caught?

This letter, taken together with subsequent events, leaves little doubt that Rob Roy was at this time, if not before, in secret collusion with Argyll.

Again, he was playing one great man against another. Argyll hated Montrose and Rob Roy, who was nothing if not an opportunist, saw the means or furthering his own vendetta with the latter. Also, Rob Roy found 'Red John of the Battles' to be a man of his own heart. Both were natural leaders and Argyll, like Rob Roy, was compassionate, hating to see life thrown away. 'Oh, spare the poor blue bonnets!' he cried at Sheriffmuir when dragoons were driving Highland men into the Allan Water to drown.

Some protagonists claim that it was Rob Roy's own hatred of seeing men killed and wounded to no purpose which made him take his stand at Sheriffmuir. Others, less charitable, claim that it was part of a pre-arranged agreement with Argyll. The fact that he was soon to seek Argyll's protection is clearly beyond dispute.

Raids in Menteith and the Lennox

At the beginning of December 1715 Mar ordered Rob Roy to take two companies of his men into Menteith and the Lennox to raid the land of Montrose.[42] In obedience to this instruction, he descended upon the estate of Auchintroig, near Gartmore, and carried off the Whig landlord, John MacLachlan of Auchintroig, and two of his sons as hostages together with most of their stock.

Montrose, who was about to become Principal Secretary of State to George I, sent naval vessels to Dumbarton. From there a hundred seamen, together with the local militia, set out to capture Rob Roy. Commanded by Grahame of Killearn, Montrose's factor, they marched to Craigrostan, where Rob Roy was thought to be, only to be told he had moved to Strathfillan. Continuing through darkness, they followed him and Grahame, told that he was sleeping in a barn at the 'change-house' or inn at Crianlarich, thought he had got him at last. In securing the doors from outside, however, the scraping of the iron bolts was enough to wake Rob Roy, who sprang to his feet sword in hand.

Grahame's men, trying to rush the door, were felled by that terrible blade. Rob Roy held them back as his followers, said to be twenty in all, broke out of the barn and fell upon the terrified militia. Grahame,

Loch Tay and Ben Lawers

Beinn Dorain overlooking Auch Glen, Argyll

Inveraray and Loch Fyne

Beinn Bhuidhe, Rob Roy's house in Glenshira

seeing they carried flintlocks, shouted to his men to run, but several were killed by gunshot before they could get out of range. The survivors fled in terror, pursued by yelling Highlanders wielding their vicious claymores.

Rob Roy is known to have left Crianlarich and continued up the road to the house which Breadalbane had given him at Auchinchisallan. The unfortunate MacLachlan of Auchintroig and his two sons, together with two other hostages, no doubt feeling themselves lucky to be alive, were forced to go with him but shortly afterwards set free. Rob Roy, apparently realising that MacLachlan's people were in want, returned to him the sheep, cattle and horses which he had taken from his land.

Falkland Palace

The next authentic evidence of Rob Roy's movements at this time is the order sent by the Earl of Mar, dated 17 December 1715, recalling him to Perth.[43] He arrived in the city just as it was known that Prince James Edward Stewart, or James VIII and III as the Jacobites claimed him to be, had actually landed at Peterhead. Before setting off to join him Mar instructed Gregor MacGregor of Glengyle, Rob Roy's nephew, to garrison Falkland Palace in Fife. Gregor took command of the castle on 4 January 1716 with a force of about 150 men. Rob Roy, who is believed to have been among them, reputedly provisioned the castle by raiding the local lands.

It being late winter, however, there was little to be had and the legend runs that Rob Roy, ever resourceful, robbed a funeral feast. The banquet was much enjoyed by the garrison and Rob Roy did return the horses which he had 'borrowed' to carry it away.

It would seem to have been from Falkirk that Rob Roy was sent by Lord George Murray to collect customs duties for King James in Fife. The weather was particularly cold and most of his men who were barefoot shivered in an icy wind. The story goes that they reached Arngask on a Sunday morning as the well-shod citizens came trooping out of the kirk. Rob ordered them down on their knees to pray for

King James and when some of them refused, he told his men to remove their shoes and put them on their own blistered feet. Then, in a further flash of inspiration, he reputedly took their bibles and forced them to pay for their return.[44]

More factually, it is known that on 20 January Rob Roy, with a force of his men, seized and garrisoned the Tower of Balgonie, belonging to the Earl of Leven, at Markinch nearby. Here he is said to have captured a party of Swiss mercenaries whom he imprisoned in the castle. He partly destroyed the building to make it uninhabitable for the enemy, before being ordered to leave.

James VIII and III, having landed at Peterhead, was now at Scone Palace near Perth. An announcement was made that he would be crowned there on the 23rd of the month but the ceremony never took place. Argyll was by now advancing upon the city of Perth and Mar removed his headquarters to Dundee. From there he issued instructions to Gregor MacGregor of Glengyle, signed at the Court of Scone on 27 January, to march with 'his battalion of the name of MacGregor' to the valley of the Teith, near Doune, to destroy the crops and drive off the cattle to prevent Argyll's army finding provisions on the march.

Rob Roy is known to have captured the grain for the garrison of Stirling Castle.[45]

Shortly after this, on 3 February, word came that James VIII and III, believing his cause to be lost, had embarked on a French ship and was sailing back to France.

Auchinchisallan

Following the dispersal of the Highland Army in March 1716, Argyll gave orders to General Cadogan, who had arrived from Ireland as his second in command, to subdue the rebellious Highland clans. Cadogan, apparently infuriated by the damage done to the Tower of Balgonie, is believed to nursed a deep hatred for Rob Roy.

Rob Roy, warned to expect an attack on Auchinchisallan (now Auch), prudently moved his wife and children to Glengyle. He then sent a message to his principal Lieutenant, Alasdair Roy, to bring more of the clan from Craigrostan to defend his house. However, they were not able to cover the distance before a party of Swiss mercenaries arrived.

Whether they were the men imprisoned by Rob Roy in the Tower of Balgonie is unknown. If so, they may have had a special reason for taking this chance of revenge. Rob Roy saw them coming up the narrow defile from Tyndrum on the track which runs close to the hill, now part of the West Highland Way. Grahame of Killearn, writing to Mungo Graham of Gorthie, the Duke's chamberlain, described what then occurred.

> The party caryed off his whole plenishing and goods, except a few wild beasts that ran away with the fyring, and burnt all his houses save one little barn. But Robert was not able to bear all this without attempting some revenge. Therefor with a few of these he could gett readiest, his Craigrostan folks not having tyme to come up, he fyred from some rocks and passes upon the partie and killed two or three . . . but all the booty was carried off. [46]

This was the second time Rob Roy had seen his house destroyed. Now, with no holds barred, in the tradition of his Highland ancestors, he showed his contempt for those who had wronged him by raiding the lands of Montrose's adherents, namely the Lowland lairds.

CHAPTER IX

Silent as Wolves in the Fold

The Raid on Duntreath – Keillie Dun

Duntreath Castle, in the Blane Valley, lies below the twin hills of Dumgoyne and Dumfoyne. Originally a fortalice of the Lennox, the tower was built by Sir William Edmonstone of Duntreath about 1452. Later, a courtyard was added expressly so that local people could drive their cattle and other animals within it when freebooters [robbers] descended from above the Highland line. Even today 'a dirty MacGregor' describes a hail or snow storm driving down from Ben Lomond and the mountains further to the north.

Grahame of Killearn, in his letter headed 'Killern, 11 April 1716' to Mungo Graham of Gorthie, was strong in his complaints: 'its most necessar you consider hou to make a new application to the Generall to take a course with these villains whose insolence is not to be born any longer. They have just now stolen a good deall of sheep of the Muir of Blane above Duntreath, and daylie threatens more mischief to all the country.'

Reputedly, the sheep in question were driven up to the old cattle stance of Keillie Dun, which lies just below Dumgoyne, from where the sons of Duntreath somehow managed to retrieve them from the MacGregors and bring them home.

The Blane Valley, wherein stands Duntreath, abounds with legends of Rob Roy. He is said to have hidden in the branches of the 'Meikle Oak', where he overheard Grahame of Killearn's men below discussing plans to take him prisoner. Sadly, the roots of this tree, which dated from the eleventh century, were severed by pipe-laying machinery. Only the stump now remains on the lower side of the road below Blairquhosh Farm.

A geological feature which forms a cave on the west side of the

Machar Glen above the village of Killearn is called 'Rob Roy's Hole'. It is said to have been one of his many hiding places in a district which, during his forays, he came to know so well.

Rob Roy's skill as a swordsman is the subject of many tales. Most famously he was challenged by MacNeil of Barra who believed himself inferior to none. Modesty in any form was foreign to MacNeil. He it was who sent his bugler to the battlements of his island fortress to proclaim 'MacNeil has dined. The rest of the world may dine also'.

This proud man is said to have met Rob Roy returning from the market at Killearn. Announcing his identity, he challenged him to a duel. The two drew their swords but after a few parries MacNeil cried out for mercy as blood poured from his arm. The gash which Rob Roy inflicted was so deep that MacNeil reputedly lay wounded in a house in Killearn for three months.

The Laird of Garden

Arguments which resulted in fighting broke out frequently in the markets and usually involved money. Rob Roy came out best on most of these occasions but in one instance he is known to have been routed by Sir James Edmonstone of Newton from the market at Doune.

History does not give the cause of their quarrel but it is on record that the Lowland landlords were by now increasingly resentful of the 'mail', demanded by Rob Roy for his services on the Watch.

One of the best-known legends about him at this time is told by Sir Walter Scott. Archibald Stirling of Garden had not paid the 'mail' which he owed. He and his wife had gone to the market at Stirling when Rob Roy arrived at the stone tower, fronted by a drawbridge, which stood near the site of the present house.

Surprisingly, the door was open and Rob Roy simply walked in to be met by a little girl who placed her small hand within his own. The two of them wandered round the house until a clatter of hooves announced the return of the laird, with his wife and their retainers from the market.

Rob Roy at once raised the ancient drawbridge which creaked up only far enough to stop Archibald Stirling entering his castle. He then held up the little girl at one of the first floor windows and shouted that he would drop her into the moat below if the money which was owed to him was not immediately paid.

The laird is said to have bellowed furiously that not a penny would he give – they could have plenty more children – but his wife became hysterical to the point where Archibald Stirling, cursing under his breath, reluctantly drew the coins from his purse.

Thus ended an episode which, if not entirely vouched for, was certainly one of the most amusing of Rob Roy's many escapades.

Arnprior

Another incident occurred near Garden in the little village of Arnprior. Here at the inn, he met Harry Cunningham, laird of the local estate of Boquhan near the village of Balfron. Harry was renowned as a dandy with lisping voice and mincing step. Also, to make matters worse, he was a Whig, like most of the Lowland lairds. Rob Roy, disliking his affectation as well as his political views, made some offensive remark to which Harry retorted in words equally rude. Instantly, both men, now fairly drunk, leaped to their feet while reaching instinctively for their swords. Rob Roy's was hauled from the scabbard as Harry, failing to find his, grabbed an old rusty weapon which the landlord kept to poke the fire. With this he set upon his opponent with such fury that, staggering backwards, Rob Roy fell upon the door. The hinges gave way with a loud crack and Rob was catapulted into the mud outside.

Doubtless, the night air sobered him for, returning to the inn parlour, he shook Harry Cunningham by the hand. With that they sat up drinking until morning, and afterwards remained firm friends.

The story, however, was too good to be forgotten and was repeated by many a fireside over the years to come.

Submission to King George I

Following the dispersal of the Jacobite Army an amnesty was declared. The men who had fought for Prince James Edward Stewart received a pardon dependent upon them surrendering their arms.

According to Rob Roy's own written account, Montrose now tried to force him by means of bribery to bear witness against Argyll. The agent he chose to make the deal was none other than Sir Adam Cockburne of Ormiston, Lord Justice Clerk at the time. Cockburne arranged to meet Rob Roy at Cramond Brig, near Edinburgh, where Rob Roy, after sending spies out to make sure he was not entering a trap, duly appeared. Details of the terms of the deal are not known, but Rob Roy, by his own word, was offered both land and security in return for a sworn statement proving Argyll's collusion with Breadalbane and other Jacobites to restore James VIII and III to the throne.

Rob Roy refused in no uncertain terms to give evidence against Argyll. Robber of cattle though he may have been, disloyalty was as repugnant to him as to most Highland people of his time. Cockburne, his mission a failure, reported back to Montrose and it would seem that word of it was soon to reach the ears of Argyll.

The Treaty of Amnesty required that Jacobites involved in the recent Rising hand in their weapons to a government representative. The fact of Rob Roy choosing to go to Inveraray to do so indicates that in Argyll's own country he felt himself to be on safe ground.

In June, he appeared in the little town with about forty or fifty of his men. Argyll himself was absent, being at that time in Carlisle where he opposed the trial of Scotsmen termed as rebels on the grounds that this was illegal in accordance with the terms of the Treaty of Union. However, Colonel Alexander Campbell of Fonab, commander of Argyll's Independent Company, was within the fourteenth-century castle and to him Rob Roy and his men gave their weapons, including, so it is said, some very rusty swords.

Fonab advised them to forthwith abide by the law. He pointed out that unarmed men had little or no protection against cattle reivers (which soon proved to be the case) and that more men than ever would be glad to pay 'mail' to the Watch. Rob Roy, who respected the judgement of this honourable man, who was also his father's old friend, might well have heeded his advice had it not been for what now had become a personal feud with Montrose.

Burning of Rob Roy's Home at Inversnaid

Following the destruction of the house which Breadalbane had allowed him at Auchinchisallan, Rob Roy had returned to Craigrostan and rebuilt, or at least repaired, what had been his own house at Inversnaid. He appears to have followed Fonab's advice by resuming his organisation of the Watch, yet it is also said that bands of MacGregor's continued to raid the local farms. Grahame of Killearn, in desperation, begged Montrose to take action and Glengyle House was burned that summer by soldiers stationed at Finlarig.

Lieutenant-General George Carpenter had just succeeded General William Cadogan as commander in chief of the Hanoverian army in Scotland and now, at the request of Montrose, he agreed to attack Craigrostan where Rob Roy was known to be. On 27 September 1716, detachments of soldiers from Glasgow and Stirling, under the command of a Major Greene, assembled at Buchanan House, owned by Montrose since the late seventeenth century.

A surprise attack in darkness was thought to be the only hope of capturing Rob Roy. Therefore, guided by Grahame of Killearn, the men marched through the night up the east side of Loch Lomond, slipping and stumbling through torrential rain. The burns rising in spate were so difficult to cross that it was daylight before they reached Craigrostan, exhausted and soaked to the skin.

Before them stood an empty house and barns. Rob Roy, warned of their coming, had sent away the women and children, driving the animals to safety while he himself had disappeared . . . or so it seemed . . .

Suddenly, shots rang out from the hill above. Several men were wounded and a grenadier fell dead. Grahame of Killearn, infuriated, for the second time put torches to Inversnaid house. The newly repaired roof collapsed and the walls once again stood blackened and open to the sky.

CHAPTER X

Rob Roy in Argyll

Glenshira

In October 1716, shortly after the burning of Inversnaid House, Rob Roy was given permission to build a cottage in Glenshira by the Duke of Argyll. The intermediary in this case was, almost certainly, Colonel Alexander Campbell of Fonab.

The house was built near the head of the glen on the east bank of the Shira river. From there it was only a short distance over the hill by the *Bealach nan Cabrach* ('Pass of the Antlers') to Brackley, the farm above Clachan Dysart (Dalmally) which he had been renting from Breadalbane since 1714. The now ruined cottage of *Beinn Bhuidhe* ('the Yellow Mountain'), named after the hill which towers above it to the north, stands close to the bank of the river. Built by Rob Roy's own men of rough stones over a framework of wooden crucks, it contained two, or perhaps three, small rooms, partitioned off from the byre at one end. The roof would have been thatched with turf or heather as was usual in those days.

Lord Archibald Campbell says that Rob Roy had the house for seven years and was popular in the neighbourhood of Inveraray town. His sporran, found in the ruin of the cottage, can be seen in Inveraray Castle, together with his letter to the Duke warning him of a would-be assassin.

Beinn Bhuidhe was not a family home. Helen Mary and the children never lived there and for Rob Roy it was a place to spend a night or two while driving cattle to and fro. Many beasts, fattened on Montrose's land, must have been held in the nearby hollow, a natural 'beef tub' where animals could be kept.

Today, the roofless, largely ruined cottage is difficult to find. Perhaps its isolation, and the encroachment of the trees, heighten its feeling of the past. Rob Roy and his gillies, their dogs beside them, might still be sitting round the central peat fire. Their Gaelic speech may just be heard in the the sound of the tumbling burn. Perhaps they are having a good laugh. Wondering if Montrose has missed his cows . . . one thing is almost certain – that each and every one will have a dram brought from a still on the side of Loch Awe, not far away over the hill.

We are fortunate that some of the traditional tales have been recorded. During his boyhood, John Ferguson, a cooper who was eighty-nine in 1882, had listened to the stories of people who had actually known Rob Roy.

'I have heard my father and grandfather speak of Rob Roy MacGregor, who used to plunder Montrose's cattle and drive them to a fank [enclosure] at the head of Glenshera [sic]. I have heard them say that Montrose wrote to Argyll accusing him of giving refuge to a robber; and that Argyll replied, "You feed him; but all he gets from me is a cave and water." I have heard my father tell a story that a stranger had entered a place where Rob Roy's band put up, and that the stranger stole a pot wherein some beef had been boiling, and ran off with it, and that Rob Roy's men pursued him as far as Dalmally and recovered the pot.'[47]

Another worthy called George Clarke, who was a keeper at Rosneath, recalled a more interesting incident.

'When Rob Roy was in Glenshera [sic], he and his gillies were setting out for a market at Fort William, through the hills by Glenorchy. He sent one of the gillies round by Inveraray for tobacco, who was to join the party at Ardhetal [Airdtheteil], in Glenurchy [sic], where they were to lodge for the night.[48] As it was late autumn, a heavy snowstorm came on.

'One Munro (some of his grandchildren are still about Inveraray) being the tenant of Carnus, the highest farm in Glenara [north side of the glen] had a heifer which had been housed the previous winter and turned out to moor-pasture in summer, and which, on account of the storm, came home and stood before the byre door. Rob Roy's gillie came to the door of Munro's house wanting lodgings for the night; and on his knocking at the door, Munro came out, when the gillie told him he was on his way to Glenurchy, but could not proceed on account of the snow. Munro refused to take him in and, not recognising the animal, asked, "Is that your cow there?"'

'The gillie replied in the affirmative and said, "Since you will not oblige me with a night's lodging, will you help me over your farm with the cow?" Munro, glad to get quit of him, conveyed him and the cow over the boundary. So the gillie drove the cow to Glenorchy where Rob and the other gillies were storm-stayed. They killed the cow, used some of it, and gave the rest to the poor people there. For the loss of his cow Munro summoned Rob Roy and his gillie before the Sheriff at Inveraray. However, the Sheriff dismissed the case and even reprimanded Munro, stating that the man might have been lost in the snow; and besides that, he himself helped to drive the cow off his own farm, and therefore had no claims against the gillie.'

Brackley

Brackley, the Gaelic name of which is *Breac-leathad*, meaning 'the Speckled Slope', was part of the land held by the MacGregors when, sometime in the twelfth century, they settled round the eastern end of Loch Awe. John MacGregor of that ilk, who died in 1461, left the lands of Brackley, together with a numerous following of men, to his second son, Gregor Mor, from whom were descended the cadet branch of the Clan Gregor. The MacGregors of Brackley held their land until 1686 when, on 28 August, John MacGregor of Brackley and his father, Patrick Graham (alias MacGregor), resigned their property of Brackley to the Earl of Breadalbane.

Rob Roy rented the farm from Breadalbane in 1714. Two years later he built the cottage at *Beinn Bhuidhe* in Glenshira just over the ridge. The two places, connected by the old road leading from Loch Fyne were only some seven miles apart. Rob Roy knew every inch of that country, still connected by legend with his name.

Coming from Glenshira he would first have reached the Tailor's Village, where people from both sides of the hill came to have their home-woven tweed made up for them to wear. Next, coming down the hill, he would have passed Barran, where now a single house stands. Still further down the hill was Auchtermally, where the people were renowned for their skill in making horn spoons. Limestone, burned and crushed, was beginning to be used as a fertiliser and the lime kiln, still containing a boiler, stands close to the burn.

In 1846 a family called Crerar rented Brackley, by then a sheep farm, from Lord Breadalbane. They bought it when most of the Breadalbane estate was sold, c.1932. Today, Mrs Sybil Macpherson works the farm – which, at near 4,000 acres carries 1,000 ewes – very largely on her own. Her father, the late James Crerar, a local historian, loved to relate the following legend about Rob Roy.

The Dinner at Barran

The old cottage of Barran, built for a shepherd where a black house once stood, lies on the farm of Brackley to the south of the village of Dalmally.

Rob Roy was returning from the market, probably driving some cows with a dog at his heels, when upon reaching Barran he saw a woman carrying water in a bucket from the burn. He gallantly offered to carry the bucket and followed her into her home, a low thatched cottage with a fire in the centre of the only room. Above the fire hung a pot from which came the most appetising smell. Rob, laying down the bucket, asked if she could spare a little of the stew. Abruptly, she refused, no doubt telling him to be gone, whereupon, infuriated, he filled his bonnet with water and dashed it over the fire. Smoke poured in all directions with a loud hissing of steam. The woman, half blinded, threw her apron over her head. When, within a few moments, she could see again, she found that Rob Roy had vanished and so had the iron pot with the dinner which had sizzled so temptingly above the fire.

This is just one of the legends relating to Rob Roy's time in Argyll, where, with this one exception, he seems to have been well received. He was certainly popular in Inveraray, as other stories denote. One concerns a funeral in which he played an important part.

A Funeral at Kilchrenan

The MacCorquodale Barons of Phantilands had long lived at Kilchrenan on the north shore of Loch Awe. In the seventeenth century they moved to Inveraray, but members of the family continued to be buried in the graveyard by the pre-Reformation Church of Kilchrenan.

In 1714, the son of Ewan MacCorquodale died and the Burgesses of the Burgh, as well as many friends and acquaintances living in the neighbourhood, received notice by word of mouth to attend the funeral. The hour fixed for the meeting at the house was shortly after one o'clock in the morning. Every custom associated with a Highland funeral was duly observed. As they arrived, people were invited to go inside and partake of the refreshments so liberally provided.

From the head of Glen Shira and from the Corran came men of daring who had in their day gloried in the fierce sound of battle, and who had faced death on many a stricken field. With them was Robert MacGregor Campbell, better known to the world in after years as 'Rob Roy'.

Unfortunately, it was then remembered that no funeral procession should start until after cock-crow, and this would appear to have been a winter's night, which meant a long wait.

> Into MacCorquodale's house the people crowded, and were served with oat and barley cakes and cheese, washed down with a plenteous supply of good whisky drawn from the sma' stills of Lochow ... all the old stories of funerals, with the different events which occurred ... were rehearsed.

At last a cock was heard to crow. The coffin was put upon the spokes (two planks of wood) and the cortège began the long walk to Kilchrenan. The bearers changed places several times and more refreshments were consumed. Portsonachan was reached, the ferry crossed, and the funeral accomplished without mishap, but then the assembled mourners departed to *Tigh-creggan* (Taycreggan) Inn. There, after several drams, a Kilchrenan man called McDiarmid, disputed the right of the MacCorquodales, who were now followers of the Chief of the Campbells, to continue to bury their dead in Kilchrenan churchyard. 'Words gave place to blows . . . Kilchrenan Inn was wrecked . . . Rob Roy and his companions were in their glory, and where the fight raged keenest, there were they dealing forth Herculean blows and knocking their opponents over by the score. Finally, the Inveraray men fought their way to the ferry and got over to Portsonachan.'[49]

This, however, was the last MacCorquodale funeral at Kilchrenan. Afterwards they were buried near Inveraray in the old churchyard of Kilmalieu.

CHAPTER XI

Revenge

Chapelarroch

Rob Roy was quick to take revenge for the burning of his house at Inversnaid. The story of how he did so is perhaps the most famous of his exploits in his war against Montrose. The tenants of the Montrose estates, as elsewhere in Scotland, paid their rent at what is still called the 'November Term'. Much of it was paid in kind, but some money also changed hands. In West Stirlingshire, for example, the farmers came in to pay their dues at Chapelarroch, a farmhouse between the villages of Drymen and Gartmore. Seated at the head of the table was Grahame of Killearn; as tenant of the farm and the Duke's factor, he collected the money and gave a signed receipt to each man. The day was always a long one as some came from afar, but the business was almost finished as darkness began to descend.

Suddenly, there were shouts of alarm from outside. Grahame, with great presence of mind, ran up a wooden stair and threw the sack containing the money into a loft above. Hardly had he done so when candles blew out in a blast of air as the door was thrust open and Rob Roy strode into the room.

The armed men with him quickly found the sack. Rob Roy opened it, took the money – which proved to amount to £3,227. 2s. 8d. Scots – and then gave or dispatched new receipts to the tenants, signed in his own hand.

Next, he turned to the luckless Grahame, ordering him to write to the Duke of Montrose, telling him he was a hostage and asking to be ransomed from captivity.

The letter, headed 'Chapelarroch, 19 November 1716', begins: 'May it please your Grace – I am obliged to give your Grace the trouble of this, by Robert Roy's commands, being so unfortunate at present as to be his prisoner.' He went on to say that all Rob Roy wanted was a discharge of all the money which he owed Montrose plus 'the soume of 3400 merks for his loss and damages sustained by him both at Craigrostan and at Auchinchisallan; and that your Grace shall give your word not to trouble or prosecute him afterwards, till which he carries me, all the money I received this day, my books and bonds for entress, not yet paid, along with him.'

The letter was taken to Montrose, then in Glasgow, by one of Grahame's men. He himself, hoisted on to a horse, was carried through Aberfoyle, up the east shore of Loch Ard and then to Loch Katrine. There, on the little island of Eilean Dhu, he was held prisoner, it would seem in a turf hut, for several days.

Montrose, on receipt of the letter from Grahame, sent out parties of horsemen to search for him but no offer of ransom money was made. Rob Roy did not treat his prisoner badly – Grahame would certainly have reported it had he done so. After some days, with no offer of payment forthcoming, the captive was taken to Kirkintilloch where, together with his books and receipts, he was released and somehow found his way over the twelve miles which lay between Kirkintilloch and his home in Killearn.

A Price on His Head

Following his capture and release of Grahame of Killearn, Rob Roy, with a price on his head, moved from place to place. He seldom stayed more than one night at a time in a house and frequently slept in caves or in a sheltered hidden place on a hillside from where he could easily escape.

In the early spring of 1716, Montrose ordered his chamberlain, Mungo Graham of Gorthie, to obtain guns and ammunition from Dumbarton Castle and distribute them among the tenants who were called to arms. Rob Roy, however, having got wind of this, raided the farms and purloined all the weapons before any retaliation could be made.

The Argyll hills of Ben Odhar, Ben Dorain and Ben a' Chasteil

Barran, near Auchtermally, in the shadow of Cruachan

Conichan in Glen Almond, a MacGregor settlement

Eilean Donan Castle at Loch Duich

Montrose set out from London in April with a well armed force to organise Rob Roy's capture himself. Heading north from Callander, on the track up the east shore of Loch Lubnaig, he met a man, who, either willingly or under pressure, divulged that Rob Roy was in the township of Balquhidder.

This time Montrose was lucky. Bursting into a house in the early morning, his men found and seized Rob Roy before he had time to grab his sword. With his prisoner in hand, Montrose was taking no chances. Remembering what had happened before when Rob Roy had jumped from the back of a horse and disappeared, he now had him mounted behind a trooper to whom he was tied with a tough leather girth.

The file of soldiers headed back towards Callander above Loch Lubnaig. This time there could be no escape as an armed soldier rode before and behind the prisoner. On the narrow track above Loch Lubnaig they could only move at walking pace until they reached a better road. On flatter ground they made faster time but, nonetheless, it was growing dark before they came to the crossing place on the River Forth known as the 'Fords of Frew'.

Rob Roy had escaped death once before at this spot when the iron plate in his bonnet had saved him from the cut of a sword. Now his mind was working furiously on ways of another escape . . .

On reaching the crossing place, he recognised a heaven-sent chance. Melting snow in the hills had turned the Forth into a torrent barely possible to cross. The ford being only just passable, the main body of soldiers went over first, the horses snorting and jibbing as the full force of the current hit them in mid-stream. Because of the obvious danger Rob Roy's hands were untied before the charger, with its double burden, was forced into the stream.

What happened next is uncertain. The soldier to whom Rob Roy was bound, a man named Stewart, may have known him of old. He possibly loosed the buckle of the girth or else Rob Roy had a knife concealed. Somehow, in the tumultuous water, in the now fading light, he slipped off the back of the horse and dived under the belly of another, headlong into the stream.

At once all was confusion. Men cursing in fury swung their horses round. Shots were fired into the river . . . Then there were yells of triumph as Rob Roy's plaid floated to the surface. A fusillade of gunfire tore the woollen material to pieces as it floated down stream. The man must be dead – no one could survive such a hail of shots – yet no sign of a body appeared.

Then, slowly, the men realised that the incredible had occurred and that once under the water he had somehow got rid of the plaid. Swept downstream by the swift current in the darkness, Rob Roy had once more disappeared.

The unfortunate Stewart, riding out of the river, was met by a furious Montrose, who, loosing control in his rage, stunned him with the butt of his pistol. His descendants afterwards claimed that he never fully recovered – such was the force of the blow.

Capture at Dunkeld

News of Rob Roy's escape from Montrose at the Fords of Frew travelled the length of the country until it reached the ears of the king.

On 16 April 1716, John Douglas, the Duke of Atholl's lawyer in Edinburgh, wrote to him to say that the Lord Justice Clerk, Adam Cockburne of Ormiston, was 'earnestly Intreating of yr Gr that you would be pleased to think upon some method whereby Rob Roy McGrigour might be brought to surrender to the Govermett'.

Atholl was placed in a predicament. He had no personal quarrel with Rob Roy, who had actually surrendered to him some twenty-two years before. Nonetheless, he was desperate to obtain the king's favour to win a reprieve for his own son, Lord Charles Murray, who had been convicted of treachery as a Jacobite and was under the threat of execution in Carlisle Jail. Atholl wrote to Rob Roy suggesting that they should meet to talk over a renewal of the submission he had made so many years before.

Rob Roy agreed to come on the condition that he was granted a safe conduct, a request with which Atholl duly complied. Thus, the elusive MacGregor arrived at the Duke's house in Dunkeld on Monday, 3 June.

Atholl asked him the same questions put by Adam Cockburne as to the loyalty of Argyll (see page 87). Rob Roy, as previously, refused to answer whereupon Atholl had him arrested and taken under close escort to his prison at Logierait.

Logierait

The old prison of Logierait stood on a hill on the north side of the River Tay, just before its confluence with the Tummel near the village of Ballinluig. Logierait House stands adjacent to the site.

Rob Roy was treated as a political, rather than a common prisoner, Atholl having given instructions that he was to be used 'tenderly'. His imprisonment, apart from the restriction of his liberty, must have seemed luxurious for, as he told the Duke, he had not spent more then three nights under the same roof in as many months.

His 'tender treatment' included the provision of a copious supply of whisky. This he shared with his jailers who evidently enjoyed the company of this now notorious man.

Adam Cockburne, the Lord Justice Clerk, writing from Edinburgh on 5 June, told Atholl, 'I cannot express the joye I was in upon' at the news of Rob Roy's capture and urged that he be taken to Edinburgh Castle for greater security.

On 6 June Rob Roy was told that a party of soldiers were on their way from Perth to escort him to Edinburgh. Sometime later in the morning one of his own men arrived, saying that he had been sent by Helen Mary, who was anxious to learn of her husband's welfare. Rob Roy was allowed to go to the door to talk to the man, one of the jailers tactfully standing aside as the messenger told and received news. As the conversation continued Rob Roy edged ever closer to the door. Suddenly, he was through it and on to the back of the strong horse on which his man had arrived.

He was away before anyone could stop him, riding flat out for Aberfeldy down a tolerably good road. Pursuit, if any, was half-hearted. The escape bears the hallmarks of having been carefully arranged. The route had been well planned. He hid first in a MacGregor settlement at Conichan in Glen Almond before moving stealthily, probably under cover of darkness, down a well-known route in Glen Quaich. From there, he found his way secretly to Balquhidder where lay one of his safest places of hiding, a cave on the Tulloch burn.[50] Its entrance is concealed by a waterfall, a curtain which in spate becomes a torrent, totally concealing it from view.

Forlorn Pursuit

Atholl made furious protests over what had occurred. Nonetheless, he was a man of honour who had given Rob Roy a safe conduct and it seems that it was only his intense anxiety to save the life of his son which drove him to comply with the Lord Chief Justice Clerk's demand. In addition to this it must be remembered that no less than three of his sons were Jacobites who must have been able to send bribes through friends in the district to the men within the prison itself. Jailers in those days were notorious for their ability to turn a blind eye. Money could open even the most secure of doors.

Nonetheless, whatever his private inclinations, Atholl had to be seen to be complying with his peers in authority who expected him to arrest Rob Roy. Therefore, on 8 June 1717 he ordered that notices should be displayed in public places through Perthshire demanding 'the apprehension of Robert Campbell, Commonly called Rob Roy'.

He next despatched Donald Stewart, his chamberlain, with a party of sixty men to search for Rob Roy while at the same time sending Alasdair Stewart of Innerslanie, in Glen Tilt, who knew every inch of the surrounding district, to make a secret solitary search.

Neither attempt was successful. The local people would not, under any circumstances, betray the man who had been a friend to so many of them in times of need.

Rob Roy himself was now in and about Balquhidder, moving from one safe house to another, or to his cave on the Tulloch burn above Loch Voil where his presence was never known. He is reported to have been ill at this time, yet on 25 June he wrote a pamphlet headed

Declaration Rob Roy to all True Lovers of Honour and Honesty.

In it he stated bluntly that attempts had been made through Grahame of Killearn and Lord Ormiston (Sir Adam Cockburne) on behalf of Montrose to betray Argyll as a Jacobite and that further to this 'His Grace the Duke of Atholl . . . having coy-duk'd me into his conversation, immediately committed me to prison, which was contrary to the Parole of Honour given to me by my Lord Edward in the Duke's name . . . The reason why the promise was broke to me was because I boldly refused to bear false witness against the Duke of Argyll. It must be owned, if just providence had not helped me to escape the barbarity of the monstrous proposals, my fate had certainly been deplorable, for I would be undoubtedly committed to some stinking dungeon, where I must choose either to rot, dye, or be damn'd.' He continues to say that 'To narrate all particulars made towards this foull plot, and the persecution I suffered by the Duke of Montrose's means, before and after I submitted to the Government, would take up too much time. Were the Duke of Montrose and I left alone to debate our own private quarrell, which in my opinion ought to be done, I would shew the world how little he would signify to serve either King or Country.'

Copies of this diatribe were sent to Montrose, Atholl, Argyll and other clan chiefs as well as to men of eminence in Glasgow, Edinburgh and even London. The reaction of the recipients is not described. It is safe to surmise that they were furious, although Argyll may have had a quiet smile.

The Cave by Loch Katrine

Throughout the autumn of 1717 the MacGregors continued to lift cattle on the lands of both Atholl and Montrose. Donald Stewart, Atholl's chamberlain, had failed to locate Rob Roy, despite the assistance of sixty men. Not only that, but it seemed that he was unable to prevent the stealing of cattle from many farms.

In the second week of September he met Grahame of Killearn, Montrose's factor, by arrangement at Lochearnhead. The two were conferring as to what action could be taken against Rob Roy when word came that the man himself was in the Trossachs, at Loch Katrine or thereabouts.

After riding hard to reach the loch, they sent men to search the banks on either side. Meanwhile, they kept together, for fear that their quarry would reverse the tables. As darkness descended, they decided to spend the night within the shelter of a cave. Some say that Rob Roy was already hiding within in it, others that he crept up upon them from outside, but, however it transpired, he relieved them of all their weapons and disappeared silently into the night before they knew what had happened.

The Chapel of St Bride

It would seem to have been shortly after this that the Duke of Atholl heard that Rob Roy was at Monachyle Tuarach, the farm he had rented for his nephew Donald in Balquhidder in 1707.

Atholl requested assistance from General Carpenter, Commander-in-Chief in Scotland, who allowed him to send a company of cavalry in pursuit of the now famous MacGregor.

With Graham of Gorthie, Montrose's chamberlain, acting as guide, a troop of dragoons dashed up the glen and took Rob Roy prisoner before he could be warned of their coming. Afterwards, they put him on a horse to convey him to prison and, with what seems like incredible stupidity, once more they left his his arms untied. This time, however, he had a stout trooper beside him as well as before and behind.

The file of mounted men made their way down the east side of Loch Lubnaig past the spot where Rob Roy had escaped before. But now the men were vigilant. There was no chance of leaping from the saddle with the soldier beside him riding knee to knee.

All chance of escape seemed to have vanished when before them they saw the Annie Straight, the place below the Annie Farm where the loch begins to narrow before its water surges down through the Pass of Leny. Below, the Pre-Reformation Chapel of St Bride stood within its churchyard by the shore . . . Suddenly, there were shouts of alarm from the leaders of the file. Probably there had been a landslide, caused by heavy rain.

Whatever had happened the track was too dangerous for two to ride abreast so the soldier beside Rob had to pull back and let him go on alone. Behind him a horse, terrified by stones slipping away beneath its feet, jibbed and refused to move. The man in front, intent on keeping his own beast on its feet, did not look round and in this instant Rob Roy saw his chance. Leaping out of the saddle, he was up the brae into thick trees, over the hill and away before the soldiers, in their confusion, had time to even load their muskets.

Once again Rob Roy was free . . .

Ambush in Glenogle

Shortly after Rob Roy's escape by Loch Lubnaig, near the Chapel of St Bride, the Duke of Atholl made another attempt to capture him with a party of cavalry. This time it was his own men, not those of General Carpenter, who rode from Glen Almond, up the Sma' Glen to Amulree, and from there past Loch Freuchie to the south shore of Loch Tay. Continuing some four miles up Glen Dochart, they then turned south to ride up to the head of Glenogle by the track which, from time immemorial, has been a main route across the hills.

From the top of the pass they looked down upon Glenogle. The heights of the hills on either side were bare save for heather, even as today, but then the lower slopes were thickly covered with birches and rowans and other low-growing trees.

Rob Roy, warned of their coming, was waiting. His men sprang out as if from nowhere as the mounted soldiers rode down into the woods where the burn narrows to a ravine. Hemmed in, unable to fire their muskets or effectively use their swords, they put spurs to their terrified horses and fled for more open ground.

Atholl, told of what had happened, seems at this point to have realised the futility of continuing to oppose a man who, largely thanks to his local popularity, had proved himself more than a match.

The Barracks at Inversnaid

Another legend linked with the name of Rob Roy at this time concerns the barracks at Inversnaid. Rob Roy's land at Craigrostan, together with other estates belonging to Jacobites, had been forfeited by the government after the Rising of 1715. It was now bought from the Commissioners of Confiscated Estates by the York Building Company, a business founded in London to take water from the Thames to York House. These entrepreneurs had purchased Craigrostan largely for the value of its trees.

The Duke of Montrose had at last received authorisation from the government to erect a barracks at Inversnaid, almost on the sight of Rob Roy's burnt-out house. The construction was under way when a party of MacGregors, reputedly sent by Rob Roy, kidnapped the builders and brought the work to a halt. The barracks were eventually finished in 1719, by which time Montrose, through the auspices of his chamberlain Mungo Graham of Gorthie, had bought Craigrostan from the York Building Company for himself.

Rob Roy did not attempt to regain the property which had caused him so much grief. The cruel usage of Helen Mary and their children by Grahame of Killearn, who had not only forced them from their home but had set fire to the house itself, was something he could never forgive. Montrose was an implacable enemy with whom he could never come to terms. Atholl, on the other hand, was a man in whom, despite their former antipathy, Rob Roy felt that he could now place some trust. Therefore, it was in Balquhidder, where Atholl as superior was in honour bound to give them protection, that Rob Roy and his family now made their permanent home.

CHAPTER XII

The Rising of 1719

Invasion

In 1717 the Spanish seized the islands of Sardinia and Sicily in preparation for an attack on the mainland of Italy. Four years earlier, in 1713, the islands had been granted to the Emperor of Austria as part of the treaty which ended the War of the Spanish Succession. Britain had been the main guarantor of that agreement and for this reason the government ordered Admiral Byng to attack the Spanish fleet in the Mediterranean. His historic victory off Cape Passaro, near Messina, resulted in its defeat.

Cardinal Alberoni, on behalf of Philip V, King of Spain, declared war on Britain and then summoned the Jacobite Duke of Ormonde to Madrid. Ormonde agreed to lead an invasion of England but suggested that it should be co-ordinated with an attack on Scotland led by the Earl Marischal, also exiled abroad. Alberoni agreed to provide enough ships to transport 5,000 soldiers and arms for many more. The fleet of about 29 ships sailed from Cadiz in March 1719. Ormonde was in Corunna when he was joined by the 'Old Pretender' James VIII and III, but here their hopes were destroyed when a few badly damaged ships appeared, bringing news that most of the others had sunk in a terrible Atlantic storm.

The intended invasion of England was thus abandoned, but George Keith, the Earl Marischal, had already put to sea with a force of about 300 Spanish soldiers in two ships. They managed to reach Stornoway in the Isle of Lewis and were joined by a small group of Jacobites who had sailed from France. Led by James Keith, the Earl Marischal's younger brother, the party included William, 5th Earl of Seaforth; the Marquis of Tullibardine (eldest son of the Duke of Atholl); his younger brother, Lord George Murray; and Campbell of Glendaruel.

From Stornoway, the ships of the expedition sailed down the west coast of Scotland and into Loch Alsh where Seaforth's castle of Eilean Donan became the Jacobite army's headquarters. But, almost as the men landed, came news of the disaster to the Spanish ships. Ormonde, they were told, would not now invade England. They must fight in Scotland on their own . . .

Eilean Donan Castle

This island castle is so often photographed that it is recognisable to people throughout the world. Today, when it stands in peaceful splendour, it is hard to imagine the roar of canons and the terror of those within who felt the building shake as missiles crashed against its walls.

In the late thirteenth century, Alexander III (1249–86) gave the land round Loch Alsh to an Irish family called Fitzgerald, people who, having changed their name to MacKenzie, built a tower house of three storeys and a garret within a massive curtain wall. A staircase from the courtyard leads upward to the hall. Here, Robert the Bruce found refuge when pursued by the soldiers of Edward I of England in 1306.

In 1509, the MacRaes became hereditary constables of the castle, a post which they hold to this day.

In 1719 the Earl Marischal sent the two frigates, which had conveyed his expedition, back to Spain. Hardly had he done so when a squadron of the Royal Navy, under the command of Captain Boyle, sailed into Loch Alsh. The unfortunate garrison of Spanish soldiers, heavily bombarded, were overcome by a storming party and forced to surrender. All the weapons and ammunition of the Jacobite armoury were taken and the castle itself blown up. Over three hundred years later, the MacRaes carried out restoration so skilfully that Eilean Donan is one of most important thirteenth-century castles, still inhabited, in Scotland today.

Glenshiel

Following the fall of Eilean Donan, the Earl of Seaforth raised a force of about 500 MacKenzies and the Marquis of Tullibardine was reinforced by a body of men recruited in Perthshire by his brother, Lord George Murray. Then the Captain of Clanranald, Cameron of Lochiel, and MacDougall of Lorn joined his standard, as did Rob Roy MacGregor with a band of his men.

Scouts came in with the news that General Wightman, a veteran of Sheriffmuir, now in command of the Hanoverian garrison at Inverness, was marching south through the Great Glen and Glenmoriston. Tullibardine advanced to confront him and the two armies met and fought in Glenshiel.

The narrow glen below massive mountains echoed with gunfire as Wightman fired a barrage from his battery of Cohorn mortars. Overcome by the onslaught, the men of the Jacobite army were driven up the slopes of the mountain ridge known as the 'Five Sisters of Kintail' on the north side of the strath. Seaforth, wounded in the leg, was carried upwards out of range of the guns by his men. The unfortunate Spaniards fled up and over *Scurr-na-Spainnteach* ('the hill of the Spaniard') and their commander, his men nearly starving, surrendered to Wightman the next day.

Before this, as night had fallen over the dead and wounded lying on the open ground, Tullibardine had disbanded his army and, together with his brother and Seaforth, had managed to reach the ship which eventually took them to France. Rob Roy, who is also thought to have got away via Glen Lichd and then by sea, took refuge in Glen Shira where he could safely hide. Montrose wrote to Argyll accusing him of sheltering 'that well-known cattle thief' to which Argyll famously replied 'You feed him. All he gets from me is wood and water.'

Red John of the Battles, about to be made Duke of Greenwich and now high in favour with King George, could afford to deliver a snub.

The Burning of the Black Mill

It would seem to have been at about this time, 1720, that Rob Roy received an appeal for help from Grant of Rothiemurchus who had quarrelled with his neighbour, the powerful Mackintosh of Dunauchtane.

The cause of their disagreement was a mill, or rather two mills. Mackintosh had recently built a new one for which, during a dry summer, he had diverted water from the burn which turned the wheel of that belonging to Grant. A furious skirmish resulted and the Grants were overcome. Rothiemurchus, holed up in his house, the 'Doune', knew that his enemies were gathering to set fire to the roof over his head and lay waste to his land.

The runner sent speeding over the Larig Ghru to find Rob Roy had not returned. Rothiemurchus, believing all hope was gone, is said to have been sitting alone in despair when a hand gripped his shoulder and he looked up to see a kilted figure, armed to the teeth, who proved to be none other than he whom he had summoned to his aid . . . At that moment a solitary piper appeared playing *The Rout of Glen Fruin* and one by one the MacGregors emerged from the trees above the bank of the Spey. The Macintoshes, terrified by the sight of them, allegedly turned tail and fled. They left the place so deserted, running to hide elsewhere, that next day the Grants and MacGregors together destroyed the newly built mill.

The reel called *The Burning of the Black Mill* is believed to have been composed by a MacGregor (perhaps the piper) and is danced on Speyside to this day.

CHAPTER XIII
Balquhidder

Inverlochlarig

The burn which becomes the River Larig rises just below the
watershed on the south-east side of the head of Loch
Lomond. Descending steeply at first, it is joined by other
streams which plunge from surrounding heights to become the River
Larig which runs into Loch Doine.

Inverlochlarig is a remote glen that runs west from Loch Doine to
Parlan Hill dominated by *Stob Binein*, *Ben More* and *Cruach Ardrain* in
the north and *Stob an Duibhe* and *Stob a' Choin* in the south. From the
glen, passes lead west to Loch Lomond and south-west to Loch
Katrine and Glengyle, birthplace of Rob Roy. To the north old tracks
cross the hills to Glen Dochart and Crianlarich – Rob Roy's old
stamping ground. Here, his last years were spent, in the epicentre of the
country that he knew and loved so well.

As with so many other glens in Scotland, the deserted aspect of
Inverlochlarig today was unknown in the past. This was once a thriving
place. The remains of the ruined farming townships of North and
South Drumlich still stand and foundations of other houses can be
traced all the way up the glen.

It is said that the coffins of those who had died in Inverlochlarig
were carried from here to the burial ground at Portnellan on Loch
Katrine. The old way to the pass between *Stob an Duibhe* and *Stob a'
Choin* involves a steep climb. The pall bearers, struggling under the
spokes, rested the coffins on flat rocks as they renewed their energy
with drams, but once across the saddle of the pass they had a grand
walk downhill following the Allt a' Choin all the way to the loch shore.

The two main burns which feed Loch Doine run from opposite
directions – the Carnaig from the north, the Invernenty from the

south. Between them lies the farm of Marchfield, its name deriving from the boundary which, in Rob Roy's time, divided MacGregor and MacLaren lands. Rob's cousin Malcolm lived at Marchfield and Big Donald MacLaren, or 'Baron Stob Chon', at Easter Invernenty. In about 1720 Rob Roy, having acquired the land of Inverlochlarig Beag from Malcolm, built a family house. It stood on the north side of the glen at a height of 450 feet above sea level on the south-east slope of *Beinn Tulaichein*.[51] In the summer, Rob's cattle grazed on the high ground, herded by women and children who slept in rough stone huts. After the autumn harvest, the beasts, now rolling in fat, were brought down to the arable ground. Most were driven to Lowland markets, while the milk cows and the young stock – largely housed in barns attached to the houses – were wintered at home. Turned out in the spring, they grazed at the mouth of the glen where the river twists through bogs to Loch Doine before being herded back to the hills.

This was the ground on which crops were then planted and hay was grown. In his later days Rob Roy was no longer so active and probably only supervised the ploughing which, as a young man, he had done himself. At busy times, however, like hay-making and harvesting, he most likely still lent a hand with jobs such as stacking and piling up corn stooks in the field. His wife, Helen Mary, an apron over her skirt and a coarse linen sunbonnet on her head, would have been with him, working herself and chivvying the younger members of the family into saving the crops upon which they and their animals depended.

The glen of Balquhidder, unlike most Scottish glens, is almost level throughout. From the head of Loch Doine to the foot of Loch Lubnaig the land falls only twelve feet. Loch Doine, only a mile long, is joined by a narrow channel to Loch Voil which stretches for about five miles between the Braes of Balquhidder. On the north shore mostly deciduous trees – oak, rowan birch and willow – now grow close to the water's edge, while coniferous forestry plantations cover most of the south side of the glen. The upper ground, green in the summer, turns gold with the autumn grass before, in the stark days of winter, it lies dull beneath the snow-covered high tops.

The village of Kirkton stands close to the east end of the loch. Taking its name from its church, it is still, as in Rob Roy's time, the focal point of the strath. The cluster of buildings on the north slope lie open to the sun. Below them, in the foot of the glen, the River Balvaig winds its way from Loch Voil to the head of Loch Lubnaig, following serpentine bends as if uncertain of its course. The fields around are often flooded because of the flatness of the ground, there being almost no precipitation to carry the water down stream.

Rob Roy, even while assiduously improving his land, continued to organise the Watch. Nonetheless, despite these peaceful occupations, the Duke of Atholl remained determined to have him arrested and held in prison to stand trial for misdemeanours in the past.

In 1720, the widow of Rob Roy's eldest brother died, and the Duke, knowing that his old enemy would attend the funeral, is said to have seized upon the chance of taking him captive as he had tried to do unsuccessfully so many times before.

The Duke, arriving with his chamberlain and a large party of men, ordered Rob Roy to surrender before being taken under escort to Perth. Rob Roy said that he must first attend the funeral whereupon the Duke, loosing his temper, aimed his pistol at his chest and fired. Rob Roy pitched forward. Women among the onlookers screamed . . . then sighed with relief as he scrambled to his feet unhurt; his life saved by the breastplate he must have been wearing. At the same moment, a very large lady married to Campbell of Glenfalloch, hurled herself like a tigress upon the Duke, pinning him below her on the ground. Reputedly, she nearly strangled him before Rob Roy himself pulled them apart. The Duke looked round, hand on his bruised throat, to see that a large number of MacGregors, wearing the Glengyle tartan, had appeared. Unwilling to risk his life further, he apparently summoned his chamberlain and retainers and hastily withdrew down the glen.

This incident, legend or truth as it may be, was apparently the last attempt made by the Duke of Atholl to lay hands upon Rob Roy.

The stories, however, abound . . .

In 1722, a family called MacIntyre, on the estate of Murray of Glencarnaig, fell behind with their rent. Rob Roy, who had a piper called MacIntyre, kidnapped the officers of the law who came to evict the family and then forced them to sign an agreement promising never to return.

A more ingenious plan was adopted to deal with the matter of the minister's stipend. The Reverend Finlay Ferguson, introduced by the Duke of Atholl in 1724, demanded a higher salary than had been originally agreed. Rob Roy, luring him into Stewart's ale-house in the Kirkton, filled him up with whisky until, when completely fuddled, the minister conceded he was adequately paid. Subsequently, however, every autumn a fat stirk and a wedder or two appeared mysteriously at the manse.

Peace in the Glen

The Duke of Atholl died in November 1724. Shortly before, at the instigation of the Duke of Argyll, Rob Roy made his peace with the Duke of Montrose.

In the same year Major-General George Wade became Commander-in-Chief of the army in Scotland. Wade, who is now best remembered for the planning and building of the military roads which opened up the Highlands of Scotland to travellers, was renowned at the time for his diplomacy in dealing with recalcitrant chiefs. Commissioned by King George I to authorise pardons to those petitioning the Crown, Wade issued instructions to this effect. On 15 September 1725, Rob Roy made his own submission. His letter is termed in phraseology so sycophantic that most historians believe it to be the work of a lawyer, appended with a signature subscribed in Rob's own hand.

The result of this petition, doubtful as its authenticity may have been, was that Rob Roy, now approaching the grand old age of fifty-four, was once more accepted as living within the law. Afterwards, he behaved so peacefully that his name hardly features in records of succeeding years.

One story, however, is told of him which reveals his astonishing hardiness even in his later years. A Lennox laird who paid 'mail' lost several of his cows. Rob Roy was summoned and agreed to find them, stipulating only that two of the laird's own cattlemen, with their dogs, went with him so that when the beasts were recovered they could

Sgurr na Ciste Duibhe, in Kintail, at dawn

Glen Lichd, down which Rob Roy fled after the Battle of Glenshiel

Loch Voil and the Braes of Balquhidder

Inverlochlarig burn tumbling off Stob Binein

drive them back home. This being agreed, the party set off with Rob Roy, to the amazement of the Lowland men, following the near indistinguishable trail of the captured herd.

Somewhere near Ben Vorlich, Rob Roy told the two from the Lennox, a man and a boy, that they would find the cattle behind the next ridge. They must single out their own beasts and, if anyone tackled them, say that Rob Roy with twenty men were within earshot and that he 'would not forgive' a refusal to release the cows. Full of trepidation, but afraid to disobey, the two crept over the hill where, as predicted, the cattle were grazing in a glen. They drove out their own with the dogs and were taking them away when a woman, screaming curses in Gaelic, sprang out like a venomous witch. She must have had some English, however, or else they could speak her tongue, for when given Rob Roy's message she departed, grumbling under her breath.

This was the story that the Lennox boy, by then an old man, told to Sir Walter Scott, remembering how Rob Roy and his gillies had escorted them back south of the River Teith. Here, on a bitterly cold night they had slept on an open moor. The Highlanders wrapped themselves in their plaids but the Lowland men had no cover of any kind. Shivering, the boy crept in behind Rob Roy's leading drover, a huge man called Alasdair Roy. Alasdair, maybe after a dram or two, remained sound asleep even as, during the night, the boy pulled most of the plaid around himself. Waking in the morning and discovering to his horror what he had done, the lad trembled in fear of a beating. However, Alasdair Roy, brushing the hoar frost off his chest and beard, merely grunted, 'a caud nicht'.

CHAPTER XIV

The Last Battle

The Baron of Stob Chon

In 1734, when Rob Roy was seventy-three, he became embroiled in one of the perennial causes of feuds in the Highlands – namely a dispute over land.

The estate of Marchfield, belonging to his cousin Malcolm MacGregor, lay beyond the head of Loch Doine. Rob Roy's own land of Inverlochlarig, acquired from Malcolm, being on its northern march.

South and west of Marchfield lay the barony of Stob Chon ('Peak of the Hound'), a place named after the mountain of that name and recently bequeathed by his grandfather to a young man named John MacLaren, who thus became the Baron of Stob Chon.

Shortly after this Rob Roy's cousin, Malcolm, having run up large debts, decided to emigrate to America, but got no further than Oban before he died. He left behind a widow and a large family of young children for whom Rob Roy felt himself duty bound to provide. So the estate of Marchfield was divided into smaller holdings to produce a greater rent. Rob Roy promised Wester Invernenty, the south-west part, to a tenant of his own choice, but before the man could take possession, it was seized by John MacLaren, Baron Stob Chon.

This was too much for Rob Roy. For all his good intentions, he could not abide such insult to his pride. He descended on MacLaren, reputedly with a hundred men, and drove him bodily from Wester Invernenty to take refuge in Stob Chon.

This was not the end of the matter, for John MacLaren, equally incensed, appealed to his wife's relations for help. He had married Beatrice, daughter of Stewart of Invernahyle, chief of a cadet branch of the Stewarts of Appin. Now the Stewarts in a body, headed by Charles

Stewart of Ardshiel (then tutor of the clan), marched to John MacLaren's aid. Joined by the Stewarts of Glenbuckie, they formed up on a field above the village of Kirkton in Balquhidder, with their backs to the Kirkton burn, where Rob Roy, at the head of his MacGregors, found himself confronted with a force of at least two hundred men.

Knowing he was outnumbered, he also quickly realised that wholesale destruction of houses and farmland would be the outcome of a battle. Also, he did not want to risk a confrontation which might result in him finding himself an outlaw yet again. Thus, to the great disbelief of his enemies, braced for the onslaught of a charge, they saw his easily recognisable figure advance below a white flag.

Most of those assembled doubted their eyes and ears as an argument in Gaelic ensued. Eventually, however, to everyone's surprise, Rob Roy conceded MacLaren's right to occupy Wester Invernenty farm. He turned, it seemed in resignation, but at that moment John MacLaren's brother-in-law, Stewart of Invernahyle, leaped forward and challenged him to a duel.

Rob Roy was famed throughout Scotland as a swordsman, but with his limbs growing stiff and his eyesight failing he could not outmatch the younger man. Wounded, with blood pouring from his arm, he threw down his sword, in acknowledgement of defeat. Invernahyle gallantly insisted that he had beaten him only on account of his youth, but Rob Roy, sheathing his claymore, swore never to use it again.

This, his last conflict, seems to have hastened his end. His wound did not heal, he was seen to be failing, and in the month of October he apparently took to his bed. But his spirit had not deserted him, physically weak as he was. Told that a visitor, who is thought to have been John MacLaren, was approaching, he ordered his wife and his sons to dress him in his kilt and plaid and carry him to a chair. There, with his pistols and his claymore beside him, he waited as MacLaren entered the house. They apparently had a short conversation before MacLaren, sensing himself unwelcome, said goodbye and left. As soon as the door shut behind him, Rob Roy summoned his sons to carry him back to bed where he lay with his eyes closed, his last energy spent.

A priest was summoned, for Rob Roy was now a Roman Catholic, having converted from the creed of the Episcopalian Church some years before. Reputedly, he forgave his enemies but then turned to his youngest son, Robin Oig, and whispered 'You see to them.' He then asked for his piper to play the lovely pibroch *Cha till me tuille*, 'I return no more', and to its haunting music the soul of this man who had known so much violence, slipped gently and quietly away.

The Church of St Angus

Saint Angus, who belonged to the early Celtic church, founded on Iona by Saint Columba in 563, is believed to have come into Balquhidder from Dunblane in the seventh or eighth century. Approaching from the east, he fell on his knees in worship on beholding the wide fertile glen. He built his oratory in the flat field just to the east of the farm building of Kirkton and is buried on the hill above on which stands the present church. A stone called *Clach Aongais*, carved with the effigy of an ecclesiastic bearing a chalice – the Cup of Salvation – stands upright upon what is believed to be the actual site of his grave. Originally, it lay before the alter of the *Eaglais-beag* ('Little Church') the chapel built in the twelfth century, perhaps in the reign of King David I of Scotland, son of the saintly Queen Margaret who brought the old Church of the Culdees within the auspices of Rome.

In 1631, David Murray, Lord Scone, who held the patronage of Balquhidder, built a new church incorporating part of the old. This gradually became ruinous and in 1855 David Carnegie, owner of the estate of Glenbuckie, built the Parish Church which can be seen today.

Rob Roy's grave lies within the chancel of the original *Eaglais-beag*. His wife, Helen Mary, is buried with him, and Calum and Robin Oig, two of their four sons, lie on either side. The medieval grave-slab, depicting an armed Highland warrior, as so frequently happened in those days, was removed for re-use from its place above another tomb. Nonetheless, it signifies the defiant and dauntless spirit of the man known to the world as Rob Roy.

ACKNOWLEDGEMENTS

So many people have helped us with advice and information that it is difficult to name them all. However, we would in particular like to thank the following for their inestimable help in covering the very wide subject of the land which, during the 63 years of his lifetime (1671–1734), Rob Roy MacGregor knew and loved so well.

Dr MacGregor Hutcheson, whose occasional papers for the Clan Gregor Society are essential to anyone wishing to explore Rob Roy's country. John and Jeanne-Anne MacNaughton, of Inverlochlarig. Trevor and Helen Baney, founders of the Dalmally Historical Society and experts on the medieval grave-slabs of the Clan Gregor in Glenorchy churchyard. Iona, Duchess of Argyll, who brought us to Rob Roy's cottage in Glen Shira and who was kind enough to write the Foreword. Sybil MacPherson (née Crerar), who accompanied us up to Barran on Brackley Hill. Sir Archibald and Lady Edmonstone, who know all Rob Roy's haunts on Duntreath! James Stirling of Garden, who showed us the site of the castle which was guarded by a drawbridge in Rob Roy's time. Mr and Mrs Peter Joynson of Laraich, whose knowledge of the Trossachs and Aberfoyle is beyond compare. Mrs Campbell of the Comer, where Rob Roy's wife, Helen Mary, was born, who took us up the hill road over the shoulder of Ben Lomond on a beautiful day in May. Mrs James Troughton of Blair Castle and Ardchattan Priory. Mrs Rae MacGregor, founder member of Inverary Historical Society and Neil Munro Society. Ken Sethi of Genesis Laboratories for high-quality film processing. Willie Fraser, Head Ranger at Kintail.

Our special thanks go to Avril Gray and Brian Pugh of Scottish Cultural Press for their constant help and meticulous work in publishing this book. Thanks also to Amabel Barraclough for her careful proof-reading. Finally, eternal gratitude is due to Eddy McGrigor for once more giving so much help and encouragement during all the research, writing and photography that such a project entails.

NOTES

1 The modern spelling is 'Dalriada'.

2 See A. G. M. MacGregor, *History of Clan Gregor*, Vol. I, pp. 16–20.

3 Ibid.

4 Adam F. & Innes of Learney, *The Clans*, Septs 7 Regiments of the Scottish Highlands, p. 323.

5 A. G. M. MacGregor, *History of Clan Gregor*, p. 21

6 Enfeoffed – to invest legally with a right of property in an estate [Law].

7 The MacPhedrans, hereditary ferrymen of the Earls of Argyll on Loch Awe, were famed for their skill in making arrow-heads.

8 Dugal Ciar is believed to have been the fifth son of John *Cham* MacGregor of Glenorchy, who died and was buried in the old Church of Dysart in 1390 (see the family tree on page 22).

9 James Graham, Earl (later Marquis) of Montrose, is known to have worn out three pairs of boots some forty years before when stalking on the hills above Luss.

10 Transept in the Collection of MacGregor of Balhaldies.

11 W. H. Murray, *Rob Roy MacGregor*, p. 89.

12 Ibid, p. 92.

13 The Royal Commission on the Ancient and Historical Monuments of Scotland.

14 A. G. M. MacGregor, *History of Clan Gregor*, Vol. II, p. 195.

15 Ibid, pp. 194–5.

16 Ibid, p. 195.

17 See Duncan Campbell, *The Lairds of Glen Lyon*, p. 61 (privately published in 1886).

18 See J. Prebble, *Glencoe*, p. 202.

19 *An Comer* (Gaelic) means 'the confluence'; several burns join here.

20 Corriearklet.

21 A. G. M. MacGregor, *History of Clan Gregor*, Vol. II, p. 205.

22 Ibid, pp. 209–10.

23 Tacksman or tenant.

24 'Chronicles of the Atholl and Tullibardine Families'.

25 A. G. M. MacGregor, *History of Clan Gregor*, pp. 276–7.

26 Ibid, p. 277.

27 Sir Walter Scott, Introduction to *Rob Roy*, p. 31.

28 R.C.A.H.M.S., pp. 231–240.

29 'Chronicles of the Atholl and Tullibardine Families'.

30 K. M.D. MacLeay, *Historical Memoirs of Rob Roy and the Clan Gregor*, pp. 69-70.

31 See *Proceedings of Society of Antiquaries*, Vol VII, p. 253.

32 Rob Roy's Declaration in MacGregor of Edinchip Papers, 1883.

33 Chartulary of Clan Gregor.

34 'Put to the horn': if a person was found guilty of a crime, the fact was proclaimed by a herald or a messenger at a public place, such as a town cross. Three blasts of a trumpet or horn were followed by the reading out of the proclamation for all to hear. If the culprit failed to respond, letters might then be issued and those to whom they were given would be required to put the accused to death. *Notable Scottish Trials*, pp. 72–3.

35 Revd Peter Rae, *History of the Rebellion, 1746*.

36 Small brass canons.

37 *The Loch Lomond Expedition of 1715*, reprinted in Glasgow, 1834.

38 A. G. M. MacGregor, *History of Clan Gregor*, pp. 286-7.

39 K. M.D. MacLeay, *Historical Memoirs of Rob Roy*, p. 108.

40 Spulzie: 'spoil'.

41 Rob Roy's letter to the Duke of the Argyll. Reprinted in the *Argyll Papers*; the original letter is in the archives of Inveraray Castle.

42 Menteith was the area round the Lake of Menteith. The Lennox was the wide stretch of land running north of Glasgow to Loch Lomond, which included the Campsie Fells.

43 See W. H. Murray, *Rob Roy MacGregor*, pp. 195–7.

44 Hamilton Howlett, *Highland Constable*, pp. 182–3.

45 Ibid, pp. 197–8.

46 Letter from Grahame of Killearn, dated 11 April 1716, *Montrose Papers*.

47 From *Records of Argyll* by Lord Archibald Campbell.

48 Actually, on South Lochaweside on the old road south-west of Dalmally.

49 From *The Barons of Phantilands or the MacCorquodales and their Story* by Peter MacIntyre, Inveraray, courtesy of Argyll and Bute District Library.

50 Rob Roy's Cave, as it is known, is shown on the front cover.

51 W. H. Murray, *Rob Roy MacGregor*, p. 237.

BIBLIOGRAPHY

Beauchamp, Elizabeth, *The Braes of Balquhidder* (Heatherbank
   Press), Milngavie, 1981

Brown, P. Hume, *Early Travellers in Scotland* (David Douglas), 1891

Brown, P. Hume, *History of Scotland*, 3 Vols, 1909

Campbell, Lord Archibald, *The Children of the Mist* (W. & A. K.
   Johnston), Edinburgh & London, 1890

Campbell, Lord Archibald, *Records of Argyll* (William Blackwood &
   Sons), Edinburgh & London, 1885

Campbell, Duncan, *The Lairds of Glen Lyon*, 1886

Dewar, John, *The Dewar Manuscript: West Highland Folk Tales*,
   Limited Edition (Glasgow), 1961

Edmonstone, Sir Archibald, 3rd Bt., *Genealogical Account of the
   Family of Edmonstone of Duntreath* (Edinburgh), 1875

Ferguson, William, 'Scotland – 1689 to the Present' in *The
   Edinburgh History of Scotland*, Vol 4 (Mercat Press), Edinburgh,
   1965

Forsyth, Revd W., *In The Shadow of Cairngorm* (The York Building
   Company)

Gillies, Revd W. A., *In Famed Breadalbane* (Clunie Press), Perthshire,
   1938

Grant, I. F., *Everyday Life on an old Highland Farm*

Grant, I. F., *Highland Folk Ways* (Routledge), London & New York,
   1961

Haldane, A. R. B., *The Drove Roads of Scotland* (Birlinn), Edinburgh,
   1997

Howlett, Hamilton, *Highland Constable* (William Blackwood &
   Sons Ltd), Edinburgh & London, 1950

Hutcheson MacGregor, Doctor A., *Rob Roy MacGregor – His
   Family and Background*, Clan Gregor Society, Occasional Paper
   No 4, 1996

Innes, Cosmo (ed.), *The Black Book of Taymouth*, The MS of the
   family notary from the Breadalbane Charter Room (The
   Bannatyne Club), Edinburgh, 1855

Killearn Trust, *The Parish of Killearn*, 1988

MacDonald. J., *Clan Donald* (MacDonald Publishers), Edinburgh, 1978

MacGregor, A. G. M., *History of the Clan Gregor* (William Brown, Edinburgh), Vols I & II, 1898 & 1901

Mackay, David N. (ed.), *Notable Scottish Trials: Trial of James Stewart* (William Hodge & Co.), 1907

Macleay, K., *Historical Memoirs of Rob Roy*, Glasgow, 1840

Millar, Doctor A. H. Gregarach, *The Strange Adventures of Rob Roy's Sons* (Sands & Co), London

Murray, W. H., *Rob Roy MacGregor* (Richard Drew Publishing), Glasgow, 1982

Nimmo, William, *History of Stirlingshire*, 1817

Pennant, Thomas, *A Tour in Scotland and the Western Isles, 1771–75*

Ramsay, A. A. W., *The Arrow of Glen Lyon* (John Murray), London, 1930

Royal Commission on the Ancient and Historical Monuments of Scotland, vol vii, *Rob Roy's House, Glenshira* (H.M. Stationary Office), Glasgow, 1992, pp. 477-8

Scott, Sir Walter, *Introduction to Rob Roy* (Adam & Charles Black, Edinburgh, 1890

Sinclair, Sir John, *Statistical Account of Scotland, 1791–99*

Smith, Guthrie J., *The Parish of Strathblane, Glasgow, 1886*

Smout, T. C., *A History of the Scottish People, 1560–1830*

Starforth, Michael, *Clan Stewart of Appin, 1463–1752, and its Unfailing Loyalty to the Royal House of Stewart*, Appin Historical Society, 1997

Wodrow, Revd Robert, *The Loch Lomond Expedition*, Original Papers in Library of Faculty of Advocates, 1834

INDEX

61, 71, 74

MacGregor, Gregor MacGregor (chief of Clan Gregor), 33, 34, 54

MacGregor, Gregor Mor, 91

MacGregor, Gregor Roy, 24, 40

MacGregor, Helen Mary, 11, 53, 71, 99, 104, 110, 116

MacGregor, Iain, 30, 45, 46, 60

MacGregor, Ian Dubh, 6th of Glenstrae, 21

MacGregor, James, 72

MacGregor, John 'Cham', 19

MacGregor, John (s. of above), 19

MacGregor, John MacConoquy, 23–4

MacGregor, John McEwan Vic Allastair, 21

MacGregor, John, 19

MacGregor, John, of Brackley, 91

MacGregor, Lt Col. Donald Glas (father of R. R.), 30, 31, 34, 38, 39, 41, 43–5, 47–8, 53, 56, 60

MacGregor, Malcolm (supporter of Robert I), 18

MacGregor, Malcolm of Glenorchy ('Lord of the Castles'), 18, 20, 23

MacGregor, Malcolm of Marchfield, 110, 114

MacGregor, Malcolm, 8th of Glenstrae, 41

MacGregor, Margaret (mother of R. R.), 30, 41, 45

MacGregor, Margaret (sister of R. R.), 30

MacGregor, Rob Roy, 11, 12, 14, 29–33, 41, 45–8, 53, 55–61, 63–6, 70–3, 75–6, 79, 80, 83, 84, 104, 107, 116

MacGregor, Robin Oig, 72, 115

MacGregor of Kilmanan, 46, 54, 55

MacGregor's Leap (Glen Lyon), 40

MacGregors of Glengyle, 32

MacGregors of Glenstrae, 20

MacGregors of Roro, 39, 74

Machar Glen, 85

MacIain, of Glencoe, 35, 42, 49, 51

MacIntosh of Dunauchtane, 108

MacIntyre, Duncan Ban, 12

MacIntyre, family of, 111

Mackay, Gen. Hugh of Scourie, 34–7

MacKenzies of Eilean Donan, 106

MacLaren, Donald (Baron Stob Chon), 110, 114, 115

MacLauchlan, John of Auchintroig, 80, 81

MacLeans, 36, 71, 76

MacNeil of Barra, 85

MacRaes, 46, 47, 106

Malcolm IV, 18

Mar, John Erskine (6th Earl of), 72, 74–5, 77, 79, 81

Marchfield, 110, 114

Mary, Queen of Scots, 74

Meggernie Castle, 42

'Meikle Oak', the, 84

Menteith, 76, 80

Menzies of Struan, 57

Menzies, James, of Culdares, 42

Monachyle Tuarach, 68, 102

Mongomery, 71

Monteith (Heads of), 76, 80

Montrose, James Graham, Marquis (later 1st Duke of), 61–3, 68–71, 80, 87–8, 95–7, 101, 104, 107, 112

Moor of Rannoch, 12, 17

Munro, farmer at Carnus, 90

Murray, David, Lord Scone, 116

Murray, John, of Tullibardine, 38

Murray, Lord Charles, 98

Murray, Lord Edward, 101

Murray, Lord George, 38, 39, 73, 81, 105, 107

Murray, of Glencarnaig, 111

Murray, William, Earl of, 18

North Drumlich, 109

Ormonde, Duke of, 105–6

Ossian, 49

Paisley Volunteers, 76

Parlan Hill, 29, 109

Pass of Chesthill, 39, 40

Pass of Leny, 58, 102

Perth, 73, 81–2, 99

Peterhead, 81

Phantilands, see MacCorquodale

Philip of Spain, 105

Portnellan, 11, 70, 109

Portsonachan, 93–4

Prince Henry (son of Charles I), 26

Privy Council, 25, 33, 46, 48

Proscription of Clan Gregor, 26, 56, 73

Queen Anne, 61–2, 65, 68, 72

Lochan on Stob an Duibhe, looking towards Ben Lomond

Rob Roy's grave